# The Prince and the Prophet

# The Prince and the Prophet
## *The Rise of Naseem Hamed*

# Nick Pitt

Four Walls Eight Windows
New York/London

© 1998 Nick Pitt

Published in the United States by
Four Walls Eight Windows
39 West 14th Street
New York, NY 10011
http://www.fourwallseightwindows.com

UK offices:
Four Walls Eight Windows/Turnaround
Unit 3 Olympia Trading Estate
Coburg Road, Wood Green
London N22 6TZ

First published in Great Britain in 1998 by Yellow Jersey Press.
First Four Walls Eight Windows printing January 1999.

Photographic acknowledgements: For permission to reproduce photographs in this book the
publishers and author would like to thank Chris Smith, Action Images, Brendan Ingle, and the
London Sunday *Times*.

Library of Congress Cataloging-in-Publication Data:

Pitt, Nick
    The prince and the prophet: the rise of Naseem Hamed / Nick Pitt.
        p. cm.
    ISBN 1-56858-130-0 (pbk.)
    1. Hamed, Naseem, 1974-  . 2. Boxers (Sports)--Great Britain-
    -Biography. I. Title.
    GV1132.H295P58  1998
    796.83'092--dc21
    [b]                                                          98-54243
    CIP

Printed in Canada
Typeset by Deltatype Ltd., Birkenhead, Merseyside
10 9 8 7 6 5 4 3 2 1

FOR JUNE

# CONTENTS

# CHAPTER ONE

## I'll Always Listen to Brendan

Naseem was gloved up ready, and Brendan was holding the pads. It was a sunny mid-afternoon in November 1993 and the gym was almost empty. Naseem was nineteen, with nine professional fights and nine wins.

'Watch this,' said Brendan, holding up the pads, one on each hand. 'Right, Naz, show him what you can do, combination, thirty-eight punches.'

Naseem stepped into range and began by slinging a left hook to the pad in Brendan's left hand. A stream of punches followed, Naseem's hands a blur as he hit the pads from all angles, both hands, straight punches, hooks and uppercuts, with a murderous right cross as final punctuation.

'All right, this time watch his feet,' said Brendan. 'Same again please, Naz.'

Naseem pulled a face. He seemed reluctant to perform to order. But he carried out the sequence again, and extraordinary it was. His feet were almost as fast as his hands. He was switching, now orthodox, now southpaw, now square-on, always on the balls of his feet, always in perfect balance.

Brendan came across and peered at my watch. 'Second hand, good, you can time it. When you're ready, shout Go!'

Naseem was beginning to look downright unwilling. Nevertheless, 'Go!' I called as the second hand passed twelve, and Naseem repeated the exercise again, identically as far as I could tell.

'How long was it?' Brendan asked.

'Eight seconds.'

'That's thirty-eight punches, with seven different foot movements, in eight seconds,' Brendan announced. 'Even Muhammad Ali couldn't do that.'

Brendan was so proud of Naseem that he couldn't help but show him off. A dozen years before, Naseem had started, like all the others, going up and down the lines Brendan had painted on the floor of the gym, perfecting his footwork, throwing single punches on the bag, then the first combination, the old one-two, repeating and repeating before progressing, because, as Brendan never tired of saying, repetition is the art of learning. Now Naseem had mastered a combination of thirty-eight punches, complexity accomplished with certainty, the boxer's equivalent of a concert pianist's finger exercises. Of course, Naseem wouldn't use exactly that thirty-eight-punch sequence in a fight, any more than the pianist would play scales in public. But it meant he had control.

'He's the one,' said Brendan as Naseem went to change. 'He can be better than Ali, better than Sugar Ray Leonard. He's learned the whole system because I've had him since he was a kid. Some of what he does is very complicated, but he can do it blindfold because he's been at it for twelve years. I had him on the pads the other day and he stopped and said I'm fed up with this, doing the same thing time after time, and I said, listen, do what I'm telling you. I've always told him we could make a fortune, if it all goes well. He could make forty million quid. I've told him. Now he says he's going to make me a fortune, and I says yes, and it's going to be appreciated. I've told him he must watch out, that the only person who will beat him is himself.

'But then he says, about the boxing and training, we're going to do this and that, and I says to him, no, don't start saying that, we're going to do this, we're going to do that; I says to him, the minute you start telling me what to do, it'll all go wrong. You've got to do as I tell you. You're paying me to get you through, to watch out for you. He has to get in the ring and fight but I have to tell him what can go wrong. I told him last year, sorry, I explained to him last year – I've got to pick my words – I explained to him that in twelve months he's going to have problems, and I told him what I would say and what he would say. I would say you're eating wrong, you're training wrong and you're sleeping wrong; and he would say to me, so what, I'm bashing everybody up and knocking everybody out. And that's what's happened. And I also said he was going to have a bit of a problem, not a lot, but a bit of a problem with his weight, and he did.'

Naseem had changed into his jeans and leather jacket. He walked out of the gym, and motioned to a battered white Austin Metro, his first car, which was parked outside.

'Jump in, I'll give you a lift up to the house. We can talk there,' he said.

When Naseem started the engine, the Metro sounded like a tractor. 'Dodgy exhaust,' he explained.

Naseem drove up Newman Road. He parked outside the shop and led the way inside, past the sweet counter and into the parlour. The carpet was rough, the furniture basic: a table and a few chairs at one end, a settee and two easy chairs at the other. On the wall was a single large picture.

'That's Mecca,' said Naseem with pride. 'My dad went there last year on his pilgrimage.'

Naseem sat on the settee, leaning forward with his hands together. He didn't wait for a question, but started to speak, slowly and quietly, accent plain south Yorkshire.

'When I started, I used to look up to those guys in the gym, guys like Herol Graham, who was British champion. They had everything, didn't they? They was always in the papers, and I'd think they're great, and at that time they was, and I'd be watching them and all the different styles, and seeing them on telly, and I thought: if I could only box, if I could only look good. I've stuck at it for twelve years and it's worked out. I've never stopped coming to the gym. It don't get boring for me because I love training, and if you enjoy what you're doing, you won't get bored with it, and to be honest I can't afford to be bored with it because it's my livelihood now, it's where I'm going to have to make a living.

'I used to get kids calling me a Paki, stuff like that. I'd always turn round and say, listen, I'm Arab me, not Pakistani. They'd turn round and say you're all the same. The ignorance of the kids at school was

3

crazy, but then I started getting known, getting in the paper, winning Yorkshire titles, winning my first national title when I was twelve, and they said, you're in the paper, you can be our friend. When you're doing well, everyone wants to be your friend.

'I used to play football, but then I got good at boxing. I found there was a craft to it. For me, it had to be a one-man sport, where it's all up to you, do or die. I made it my dedication and determination.

'My education wasn't that good. When I came to about sixteen, I took two exams and then left school. Brendan knew a guy who got me a job as a telephone engineer. Everyone else was still at school and I was getting money and I thought I was clever. I should have stuck at my education but everything was boxing, boxing, training every day.'

One of Naseem's older brothers, Nabeel, walked in and Naseem introduced him. Nabeel, tall, slim and serious, had boxed as an amateur but had not turned professional. He was training to be a car mechanic. Nabeel sat down. 'Naz is arrogant in the ring, but not outside it,' he said, smiling.

With Nabeel beside him, Naseem resumed. 'My family has always encouraged me, especially my father. My family thinks I'm exceptional. I always wanted to be different from the other fighters in the gym. People used to say that everybody from Brendan Ingle's gym were just back-pedallers, they only know how to fight going backwards. Me, I can fight going forwards or backwards. I really started making my mark when I started banging. If I know I can go out there and knock a guy out with one shot, believe me I'll go out there and knock him out with one shot. There's no way I'm waiting around and holding anybody up. It's not my game. If I can go out and destroy him in one, he's going in one. Mind you, the second is a great round for me. You go out in the first round, you test the guy out, you look good, you pose, you do what you want. Second round: business. You go out and you destroy your man. You go out and get rid of him.

'You see, I don't want to box more than two rounds. Brendan says to me, next fight you do this, you do that, you're boxing eight three-minute rounds. I says, I'm not boxing eight three-minute rounds. He looks at me as if to say, what do you mean? I says, I'm not boxing eight threes. He says, I know you'll do him before that, and I says I know I will, I'll do him in two rounds.

'I listen to Brendan. I'll always listen to Brendan. He's been the main, key thing of the whole job. He's always said listen, you've got to listen, and he's shown me what's happened to Herol Graham and other fighters. I've seen all the mistakes. I've seen a lot of people come in and corrupt the gym and I've seen how they did it. I've seen fighters get their heads done in at different stages of a fight, and before a fight, such little things that can do a fighter's head in even before he gets in the ring. It can't happen to me. I won't allow it.

'When I get to a fight against a kid who can really fight, at the end of the day it's who's got the heart and who's got the skill. When that happens, I've got to pull through. I have to have the heart and courage to make my opponent back up, to pull me through the fight.

'When it comes to that stage, I've got what it takes. I can box southpaw, orthodox, I can switch-hit, I can dance, I can go forward. I'm an attacking counter-puncher and a good body-puncher. There's no way the guys in Britain can click on or suss me out, because, believe me, to suss me out they've got to be really good. Most of the kids are just one-dimensional. They might be good but they don't know how to express themselves in the game. I know the perfect way to express myself, and how to feel good when I'm doing it. When I get in that ring, it's not an act, it's natural, a natural me.

'The kids I'm fighting now, I'm going out there and overpowering them with my strength. But the real good kids I'll be facing in the future, I'm going to do them mentally. Mentally, I can beat an opponent and I'm going to have to do it that way. There's going to be good kids coming along – Mexicans, Americans. Bring them on. I can't wait for them because that's the only way I can prove myself and show my best ability, how good I am. It's only going to get better. There's no way I can go down. I'm going up. You came to see me when I had a Metro with a dodgy exhaust. I will be very rich. I will change British boxing and I will be better than anything that has gone before.'

5

# CHAPTER TWO

## In the Beginning

Brendan sat alone on the top deck of a number 94 metropolitan bus. It was the spring of 1981. The bus lumbered up the steep hill of Newman Road in Wincobank, a rough-and-tumble quarter perched above the old steel town of Sheffield.

He was on his way to do some shopping at Firth Park and had just boarded the bus. Now he was looking idly out of the window. Brendan liked sitting on buses. A few minutes with nothing to do, no phone, no one to speak to, just his thoughts and the world to watch. It wasn't often he had time to think. Sometimes, if he had a worry, he would get up before dawn and walk into town. He usually had something worked out by the time he got home.

The bus stopped. A couple of cars were parked outside the primary school, and the driver had to wait until the way was clear. Brendan glanced down to his left, into the school playground. Breaktime – the asphalt was swirling with kids. A commotion, a fight!

Four of them, three against one. Three white kids against a Pakistani, right by the school entrance, and the Pakistani's much smaller than the others, he's six, maybe seven years old, and he's got his back to the wall. It's not fair, but hang on, he's moving left and right, he's getting out of the way and he's throwing punches from all angles – that's it! – he's doing all right, he's holding his own, dishing it out.

It was the briefest episode, ten seconds at the most. The bus moved on, groaning up the hill. Brendan turned his head, but the playground and the fight were out of sight.

When Brendan came back on the bus almost to the bottom of Newman Road, he clambered off, walked the few yards to his house, along the side passage to the front door, and into the kitchen. Alma, his wife, was at the sink, washing up.

'Alma, I've seen this kid,' Brendan said. 'Up the road, in the school, a Pakistani kid I think, and he can fight. I tell you, he was moving, slipping, he can really fight.'

Brendan couldn't pass a fight – outside a pub, in the street – without stopping to watch. He was a student of fighting, a fight-spotter.

Alma carried on at the sink. 'I'm fed up with listening to you always going on about fighting,' she said.

About a week later, in the morning, Brendan was walking down Newman Road. He was opposite the primary school, going past the shop. It was a corner shop (except there wasn't a corner), the kind that sells most things – food, cigarettes, sweets, papers.

The owner of the shop, Sal Hamed, saw Brendan and came outside. 'Brendan, can you do me a favour?' he said. 'I'm having terrible trouble with my boys. They're always fighting: fighting at school, even in the shop. They get called names, they get picked on. There's always trouble. Look, can you wait here a minute?'

Sal went back inside and nipped behind the curtain that separated the shop from the family home. He returned a minute later, three of his boys trooping behind. Sal lined up his sons, outside by the shop window, in order of age and height.

'There they are, Brendan: Riath, Nabeel and Naseem. Can they go down to the gym? Can you teach them to box?'

Brendan looked at them. One, two, three. That was him. The smallest, the one called Naseem, that was the boy he'd seen in the school playground, the boy who could really fight. Brendan had got one thing wrong, though. The boy who could fight wasn't a Pakistani. Sal and his family were Arabs. They were from the Yemen.

Naseem looked up, unblinking. He was tiny, four foot nothing and three stone something, with big ears. A bit cheeky.

'No problem,' said Brendan. 'Send them along.'

# CHAPTER THREE
## The Treasure-Cave and Kingdom

Naseem, aged seven, along with his two brothers, pushed open the heavy black door that guarded Brendan's gym, crept up the passage, and entered a room of wonders. Music: a black ghetto-blaster was parked against the wall, gushing a throbbing reggae beat. Movement: one man was shadow boxing, another tough-looking guy slammed his fists into a punch-bag so that it swung violently on its chain. Boxers moved up and down the room, heads bobbing, hands held out in front of them. All sorts were there: blacks and whites; fighting men in their prime, their bodies hard, their legs slim and shiny; kids, tearaways from the council estates; an old man, a shuffler with spindle legs, sweating and panting as he tapped his punch-bag.

Up at the far end was the ring. It was raised, about three feet above the floor. Half a dozen boxers were sparring in pairs in the ring while others watched, leaning on their elbows and gazing under the bottom rope.

Brendan sat on some wooden steps up by the ring, presiding. A long buzz sounded from a clock on the wall. 'Time!' Brendan called. The boxers stopped sparring and walked around in a circle, like racehorses in the parade ring. The hand of the clock swept slowly round. It was a special clock, divided into four segments like a maths puzzle, one quarter in red, the other three-quarters in black. Three minutes to fight and a minute to rest. 'Change over,' Brendan instructed when the minute was up. The boxers sought out new partners for the dance and touched gloves. 'Away you go,' Brendan called, and the sparring started again.

Even when sparring was going full pelt, Brendan, from his perch on the steps, kept half an eye on what was happening around the gym. He saw Riath, Nabeel and Naseem edging along the wall, and went down to intercept them. 'Right, you three stand there by the radiator,' he said. 'Keep warm and just watch what's going on. I'll get you started later on.'

The radiator was halfway up the room, where the floor training and bag work were going on, but Naseem had his eyes on the ring and the one boxer he knew by name, the main man, Herol Graham. Bomber was his nickname, Bomber Graham. He was always in the papers; not just the *Star* but the national papers as well. In his last fight, at the City Hall, he had won the British light-middleweight title. Bomber was special, in a different class, moving so easily, gliding sideways as if he was on castors, then darting in to punch his sparring partner and slipping out of the way again. He always seemed to know what was going to happen before it did.

The next day, Brendan got Sal's boys started. They were wearing their street clothes – jeans and trainers – but that didn't matter.

'Right,' said Brendan, 'you see those lines?'

Three sets of blue lines, painted as thick as road lines on the parquet, ran from the ring down to a huge cracked mirror at the other end of the gym. Each set had three parallel lines: two solid lines a couple of feet apart and a dotted line in the middle.

'Watch me,' said Brendan.

He stood at the end of one set of lines, his hands held in front of him, ready to box, his left foot just ahead of his right, one on each solid line.

'Watch my feet.'

He stepped forward with his right foot. It hit the line again. Then a half-step with the left, on to the broken line. Then another step, with the left again, back on to the solid line. Then a half-step with the right foot on to the broken line, a full step and back to the beginning.

'Right, now you try.'

Sal's boys lined up and tried to repeat Brendan's steps. They messed it up – everyone did, first time – and Brendan showed them again, slowly, one step at a time. Pretty soon, they just about had it, but it was a stumble because they had to think about every step.

'Now, go up the line doing the steps until you get to the end,' said

9

Brendan. 'Then turn round and come back again. When the buzzer goes, go up and down for three minutes, then when it goes again, rest for a minute. Then start again. It's boring, but you've got to do it. Right, away you go.'

Naseem wanted to hit a punch-bag, so he did the steps for three minutes, and when the buzzer sounded he gave one of the bags a whack. Brendan saw it.

'No punching the bags yet,' he said. 'You have to get your feet right. You have to learn the steps first.'

Naseem had found his treasure-cave and kingdom. At school, he couldn't wait for the last bell. He'd rush home, grab his football shorts and T-shirt, and head down the hill to the gym. He did the footwork: first the simple forward steps, then advancing and retreating. He learned the split step. He went up and down the lines until he could do the steps without thinking, hit the lines without looking at his feet.

When Brendan reckoned a pupil was foot perfect on the basic steps, he moved them on to the circles. These were painted red, three sets again, outer and inner. The outer set had the same circumference as a boxing ring. Naseem learned the side-steps, round the outer circle to the right, then to the left, and he had to learn to shuffle, splitting the red line.

'I know it's boring,' said Brendan. 'I know it does your head in, but you've got to do it.'

Naseem followed Brendan's instructions, but he did his own thing too. He would hit the bags whenever Brendan wasn't watching, or wasn't in the gym, and he was always up by the ring, watching the sparring. Naseem pestered Brendan to let him have a go in the ring. After a couple of weeks, Brendan relented and at last Naseem had his chance. He borrowed a pair of gloves and jumped up under the bottom rope. There was give, a little spring in the canvas. It wasn't like moving on the floor. He was boxing against Herol Graham, the British champion – except he wasn't alone and he wasn't really boxing. Brendan had put Naseem in with a couple of the other kids, to chase Herol around. For the kids it was learning through play, and it didn't do Herol's reflexes any harm.

Naseem went after Herol and Herol slipped easily away with a laugh. The smallest kid in the gym, a third his weight and half his height, was hardly a problem. Naseem swung and missed and missed again, but kept trying, and he was moving pretty well, getting closer to landing a punch than the others. Brendan let the kids spar against each other, just to the body, no blows to the head. He sat on his steps and watched. Naseem was in with a lad who had been boxing a while and he was dominating him, hitting him whenever he wanted and getting out of the way as well.

There was something about this kid, Naseem. Brendan had seen it when he was on the bus, that glimpse in the playground, and he could see it now. It was not just his movement. That could be taught. It was something that Brendan knew couldn't be taught, something that all the champions had. Without really being aware of it, Brendan had been looking for it for years, as kids came to the gym and went away again, or came and stayed. Part of it was courage. When Brendan saw a brave boxer he used to say, 'You've got to kill him to lick him.' But it was more even than that. It was pride and a sense of territory, and maybe cruelty, too. It was fighting instinct.

# CHAPTER FOUR

## The Third Button on the Waistcoat

Brendan, ten years old in 1950, lay late in bed. He was alone. His brothers were up, all of them gone to work or school. He heard steps on the stairs, fast, urgent, and he was fearful for he knew what they meant. Jimmy, his eldest brother, nineteen years older than Brendan and a professional fighter, a famous man, marched in, yanked the bedclothes off and grabbed him. It was no use resisting, no use pretending. Brendan had been mitching off school: getting ready in the morning, leaving the house and then hiding his bag and books and going down to the seaside or the park until it was time to go home. Jimmy took hold of Brendan and beat him with his hands, beat him to hurt. Nor was it any use Brendan appealing to a bond between brothers. Jimmy was more like an uncle. Brendan was afraid of him and took his pain, waiting for the blows to stop.

'Now get dressed,' Jimmy ordered.

Head down, Brendan quickly put on his clothes and got grabbed again and dragged downstairs. Jimmy put Brendan on the crossbar of a bike, wheeled him to school and marched him straight into the classroom, Brendan squirming. Jimmy said to the schoolmaster, Mr Murray: 'He won't miss school again.'

Brendan was born and brought up in Dublin. His mother, Sara, was born on the same day as Elizabeth, the Queen Mother, 4 August 1900. Her maiden name was Lawless. She gave birth to fifteen children – the first, Jimmy, when she was twenty, the last at forty-four. Brendan was born in 1940, and in his first years there was deep sadness in the house. A daughter, born next after Brendan, died when she was three days old. A year later, his brother Joe died, aged seventeen. He had suffered from rheumatic fever, which affected his heart.

Brendan's mother went to mass six days a week, at ten o'clock every day except Saturday. On Sundays Brendan had to dress up to go to church, and also went on the first Saturday of every month, for instruction. He wasn't having it on Saturdays, so he just pretended to go. If God is so good, Brendan used to wonder, why are we skint?

Charlie, Brendan's father, was strict. He used his belt. He was called Hoppy because his right leg was an inch shorter than his left and he limped. He suffered pains in his legs and when he got home from work Sara would massage them with Sloan's Liniment. Charlie, like his father before him, began his working life as a labourer in the docks, unloading grain ships, carrying sacks that weighed two hundredweight. Later, he set up his own business as a carter, operating horses and drays. He loved horses, and when petrol-engined lorries took over, he wouldn't change with the times and was left behind.

The Ingles, father, mother and thirteen children, lived in a two-bedroomed house, 23 Margaret Place, Bath Avenue, five minutes' walk from the docks. The three girls, Bridget, Marcie and Patricia, had a settee bed downstairs in the parlour. The boys shared two double beds, four in each bed, two at each end, with a bunk bed for the others. The family ate at a long table, with Brendan's father at the head. The girls served. Only ten could fit around the table squashed up, so the rest had to eat afterwards. There was meat every day, but not much. 'Like it or lump it,' their mother would say. 'Some poor people have nothing to eat.' The boys stole each other's food, and Brendan adopted a defence that became the habit of a lifetime: eating with his head down and his arm curled around the plate.

Away from the house, Brendan had glimpses of happiness. His oldest memory was not of Joe's death, but of when he was three, barefoot in summer in the River Dodder up by Ballsbridge, with his brothers Bernie and Peter, catching pinkeens. When Brendan was a bit older, they would shin over the walls at the posh houses and rob the orchards, or stand around outside Kennedy and Nolan's, the pub at the end of the street.

'Mind your bike, Mister?' 'Yes' cost the man a penny. 'No' and his tyres were let down. In winter, Brendan earned a few pennies taking turf, for burning, round to the old people, on a barrow. There was

13

pitch and toss on every street and a card school. When she had funds, Brendan's mother gave him pocket money, fourpence a week. He'd go to the pictures, tuppence a time, at the Regal at Ringsend or the Ritz at Sandymount.

School was torture. To Brendan, a bad reader and speller, numbers were a mystery. He was in the dumbers class.

The man who changed Brendan's life was Dan Stewart, who taught him to box. Dan's proper name was David, but he was always called Dan. Born in Edinburgh around 1880, he had been a professional fighter who first fought bare-knuckle. In the Great War, he served with the Black Watch. A mortar bomb exploded in front of his trench, killing most of the men around him and leaving him badly wounded. Dan Stewart always reckoned it was the fitness he had built up training for the ring that pulled him through. He married an Irishwoman and settled in Dublin, living with her family on Londonbridge Road. Dan was a man who liked to think: he won the Irish draughts championship, and he could beat almost anyone at chess. He was tough, too, a short, strong man who could handle himself. If there was trouble in the pub and someone took him on, he always used the same move. He'd duck to his right and bring up the left uppercut. 'I hit 'em on the third button of the waistcoat,' he used to say. 'That always takes the wind out of 'em.'

Dan Stewart first arrived at the Ingle household before the Second World War. He came to talk to Brendan's father about racing pigeons, which they both kept, but they soon moved on to their other passion – boxing. They built a small gym in a shed beside the house, and Dan started training the eldest son, Jimmy. In 1939, when Jimmy was seventeen, he won the European amateur flyweight title when the championships were held at the new National Stadium in Dublin. He was the first Irishman ever to be champion of Europe, a national hero.

Dan Stewart trained all the Ingles: eleven brothers, eleven boxers, the fighting Ingles. Footwork was the key to boxing, Dan Stewart reckoned, and it could be practised anywhere. He used to say to Brendan: 'I've just been down Grafton Street, slipping my feet and dodging them all with the double shuffle.' Once, Brendan went to watch, making sure Dan couldn't see him. It was true. Dan Stewart, in his black boots, baggy trousers and bowler hat, did his shuffle and the crowd parted in front of him so that he could glide straight ahead.

Another time, Brendan and Dan were walking together in town when Dan suddenly stopped on the pavement.

'Right, Brendan, how many counters are there in boxing?' he said.

'Three.'

'Right. Always remember that. Now, what's the first?'

'The stop counter.'

'And what is that? Exactly, mind.'

'It's when you use your left hand to block a punch and move off.'

'And what's the next counter?'

'The time counter.'

'And what's that?'

'That's when you slip his lead and hit him as he comes on to you.'

'That's right. Remember, if a car hits a wall at forty miles an hour, the impact is forty miles an hour. But if the same car hits another car going at forty miles an hour in the opposite direction, that's an impact of eighty miles an hour. Now what's the third counter?'

'The delayed counter.'

'Explain that to me, Brendan.'

'The delayed counter is when you jab at a fellow, then you pull back, let him lead and hit him.'

'Correct, and it's a terrible punch to get hit with. You know, sometimes people do these counters by accident. They don't know what they're doing. But if they learned them and understood them, then they would master the art of boxing.'

In the shed next to the house were three punch-bags, a mirror and enough room for five Ingles to train at any one time. Dan Stewart had his own methods and he made it a rule that spectators were not permitted. He taught footwork on straight lines, using the gaps between the floorboards, and he taught combinations of blows to be repeated in every session.

The Ingles had a reputation. Amateur boxers in Dublin who were drawn to fight an Ingle, any Ingle, knew they'd better watch out. Once, two Ingles almost ended up fighting each other. Brendan entered the senior youth championships in March 1956 at ten stone. His brother Peter, a year older, but lighter, was supposed to fight at nine stone, seven pounds. But Peter spent the afternoon at the Carlton picture house and pigged himself on sweets and ice-cream. At the weigh-in, he was overweight, so he was put in the same division as Brendan. That night at the National Stadium, Brendan got a bye and Peter won, which meant they were both in the semi-finals. If they both won the next day, they would meet in the final, Ingle v. Ingle. Family conference. Jimmy reckoned they should go ahead – they were always fighting anyway. That was true enough. Brendan and Peter had been scrapping all their lives. But Nago (Ignatius) and Bernie were against it. It wasn't right for brother to fight brother, and what if one of them was hurt? Mother started crying, and Father put an end to it. They both scratched.

When Brendan was fifteen, Dan Stewart, who was getting on in age by then, said to him in the gym: 'Brendan, I want you to write this down.'

Dan recited from his old notebook, which was falling apart, and Brendan took dictation on a piece of paper. Later, he copied it into his scrapbook, in ink. That was one thing he had learned at school. His spelling and punctuation were not the best, but his writing was neat.

Speed in Boxing means you can see an opening Hit! The quicker you hit the speedier you are. Speed invokes three essentials quickness of (eye) to evade quickness of (mind) to decide, and speed in delivery.

Blows, By practising blows and consentrating on what you are doing improve these three essentials, beside your timing and judging of distance. Put it all in to your work when you are training and fighting. The shortest distance between two points is a straight line, and a straight punch will always arrive before a hook or uppercut.

Brendan then wrote down the exercises he and his brothers had followed for years: the individual blows, the counters, the combinations, the sequences for advancing, for moving to the right and left, for retiring or milling on the retreat. He noted the breathing exercises, the body exercises on the chair and the marks to hit for and to guard: chin, liver, stomach, heart.

The scrapbook, Browne's Scribbling Diary for 1949 (a page to each day, including Sunday), price 10 shillings and 6 pence, was Brendan's prize possession. He had started it off by pasting in newspaper reports of Jimmy's fights as a professional. Then, when he started fighting himself, he used it to keep his own record.

First entry:

February 1956, 10-stone Junior Youth Championships, first fight knocked out Hickey first round; second fight knocked out Hardgrove first round; third fight beat Byrne points; fourth fight lost Upton points.

Second entry:

March 1956, 10-stone Senior Youth Championships, Dublin Juvenile semi-finals, P. Ingle v V. Ryan, B. Ingle v B. Humstan, Row in the Camp – Nobody Boxed.

Next entry, Brendan's training schedule for the Irish Junior Championships of 1957:

November 1st to 30th. At 6.30 am run to tower and back, it is about 3 to 4 miles, come back and go to bed get up about 11 am and do the exercises till around 12.30 and for the other half hour I do footwork at 1.00 I have my dinner after dinner I rest till about 3 pm and then I go for a walk out to Merrion gates, when I come back it is about 5pm, I have my tea after that I rest till around 7pm I train from 7pm till 10pm and I finish off with the chair exercises.

17

Brendan always kept the scrapbook safe. Today it is in his kitchen in Newman Road. It measures twelve inches by six and has a faded brown cardboard cover. In it are the drills that Brendan followed himself, and later taught.

There would be many refinements, but Dan Stewart laid the foundations of the system. Dan Stewart was dead before Naseem was born. But a teacher can touch many lives. If the seven-year-old Naseem had been transported back to Dublin in the 1950s and had paid a visit to the gym in the shed at the Ingle house, and seen the brothers training on the lines and on the bags, he could have joined in, knowing exactly what to do.

# CHAPTER FIVE

## Boxing Can Damage Your Health

Brendan went to live in Sheffield in 1958, when he was eighteen. His brother, Eddie, already lived there and when Eddie came home to Dublin at Christmas, Brendan noticed the suit he wore and the money he had to spend. So he joined him, finding work first as a smither's striker in the steelworks, later as a gardener with the parks department and later still as a building labourer. He joined an amateur boxing club, Croft House, and spent his evenings listening to live jazz.

One Friday evening in 1960, Brendan met Alma Chaloner in a jazz club in the Earl Grey pub on London Road. Jazz was all they had in common: she was educated, he was semi-literate; she was a skilled chemical analyst, he was unskilled; she had lived in Yorkshire all her life, he was an immigrant; she was an English Conservative, he was an Irish republican socialist; she was Protestant, the secretary of the parochial church council, he was Catholic; she knew nothing about boxing, he thought of little else. They were married in St Thomas's church, Newman Road, on 5 August 1961.

None of Brendan's family was invited to the wedding. Three years later Brendan said he wanted another ceremony, in a Catholic church, because he didn't feel they were properly married. 'You can think what you like,' Alma said. 'As far as I'm concerned, we're married.' But they did have another ceremony, in St Patrick's, Sheffield.

Brendan went to work, and mended shoes and cut hair in his spare time. But money was short and in 1965, the year the first of their five children was born, Brendan took out a licence as a professional boxer. With the right trainer, he later liked to think, he could have gone to the top. But he trained too hard, running before he went to work and sparring in the evening when he got home. He used to fall asleep over his dinner. His ring career had no planning. He'd be rung up at short

19

notice and asked to fight as a late substitute, usually against some young full-time professional being carefully assisted up the ladder.

The vicar at St Thomas's, Fred Herrington, let Brendan use the church hall for his training. In the days when Wincobank was a village, the hall was the local school but since then it had been under-used. Sometimes Brendan would arrange for other boxers to train with him, but when no one else was around, he'd spar with his mongrel dog, Tim. It was movement, footwork, that Brendan wanted to practise, and Tim knew what to do, jumping up at Brendan, barking, snapping, moving this way and that. Tim would go with Brendan on his morning run along Underwood Bottom and Bellhouse Road. When other dogs came out barking, Tim would see them off. When Brendan sang in the house, 'Danny Boy' or an Irish rebel song, Tim howled, and he had a different howl for each song. One day when Tim was old, he went running with Brendan, but when they were nearly home Tim flaked out and Brendan had to carry him back to the house. He laid him in the living room on the rug, where Tim died. Brendan buried him in the churchyard garden.

Brendan sparred with Alma as well. When she put on boxing gloves and took a swipe at Brendan he wasn't allowed to hit back, but had to block and slip out of the way. She wasn't bad: more than once she tagged him, usually with the right hand. Brendan followed the exercises dictated by Dan Stewart, adding his own record and his own cuttings to the scrapbook.

In 1966 Brendan went over to Belfast to fight Billy Turkington in the Ulster Hall on a show promoted by Barney Eastwood, a millionaire bookmaker. The first punch from Turkington thumped Brendan between the eyes and broke a blood vessel high up on the bridge of his nose. Brendan lay on the canvas on his back, the referee counting, the crowd shouting, and blood spurting upwards. As he lay there under the bright lights Brendan had a dreamlike experience: he was in the ring, but he was swimming. The next day, his nose was a huge fleshy pulp, his forehead bruised black-purple, and he could see only around the edges of the swollen, painful mass. He arrived at work to a chorus of jeers. What a boxer, what a master of the art of self-defence!

On the building sites the worst taunters were the hod-carriers. In time, Brendan worked out how to deal with them. He had to do it every time he moved site. Right, Brendan would say, let's fight. I won't hit you because I'm a pro, but if you knock me out I'll give you a tenner. That was half what Brendan was earning for a seven-day week, twelve hours a day. Brendan would slip and duck as the hod-carriers swung at him. Men who don't know how to fight can be dangerous because their moves are unpredictable. And these were strong guys. But they were also big drinkers and as they wore themselves out, Brendan would move into range, pull them and turn them, mess them around. But he wouldn't hit them. After a few minutes they were panting wrecks. Then Brendan would say to the onlookers: 'Look at him, he's beaten and I haven't even hit him yet.' After that, he had respect.

Seven years after the Turkington fight, on 3 July 1973, Brendan had his best win. He went back to Dublin, aged thirty-three, and fought Joe Gregory, a South African ten years younger than Brendan and moving up the rankings. With many an Ingle in the audience, Brendan was cut in the first round, looked urgently for a knockout punch and found one, a left hook to the jaw, in the third. When Brendan saw the British rankings in *Boxing News*, he found that he had moved up to number eight in the middleweights.

Like many in the neighbourhood, the vicar of St Thomas's, Fred Herrington, knew that if something needed doing, it was best to ask Brendan: he never said no. Fred was worried about the youngsters who hung around the streets with nothing better to do than wait to become unemployed, so he asked Brendan to start a youth club. To begin with, Brendan set up a record player and ran dances in the hall on Saturday nights. The older boys used to fight in the street afterwards, always over girls, and Brendan took them back inside the hall, gave them each a pair of his old boxing gloves, and refereed their fights. The boxing was popular and Brendan decided to stick to what he knew. He started to give lessons.

Over time, Brendan's gym – which according to the notice by the heavy black door was both a Club for Boys and Girls and the Sheffield School of Boxing – became an extraordinary amalgam. It reflected Brendan's willingness to embrace all-comers and to teach them not only the skills of boxing but also what he called the skills of life. It was an amateur boxing club and a professional boxing gym of the kind which since Regency days has commonly been found in upstairs rooms above public houses. It was a youth club to which social workers and harassed parents directed disturbed and disturbing children. It was a keep-fit club. It was a boxing gym and an anti-boxing gym, for on either side of the ring Brendan had screwed to the wall two big identical notices: BOXING CAN DAMAGE YOUR HEALTH.

Gradually, by begging and borrowing, the gym was equipped. Brendan painted the lines on the floor for the footwork exercises. The ring was donated and erected. One famous day, three steel girders, weighing over a ton and a half apiece, arrived. It took twenty-four people to lift them off the lorry and feed them through the holes they had hammered through the wall. Some of the helpers had to rush inside and stand on chairs on tables to pull the girders across to the holes in the opposite wall. What would have happened if the tables had collapsed under the weight didn't bear thinking about. The girders were mounted ten feet up, wall to wall, so that heavy bags could be hung from them. Somehow the job was done, and with the girders being donated, it didn't cost a penny.

Brendan's own career as a boxer was over. Number eight in the rankings was the highest he would achieve. He never gave up the conviction that he could have made it to the top if he'd been able to box full time, if he'd turned professional earlier, if his career had been better organised, if he'd had a proper chance . . . But the truth was that his real career in boxing was just beginning, for what he knew he could teach, and as a teacher he had a gift that would not be denied, whatever the setbacks. If he couldn't get to the top himself, he would take others there. Brendan was in his gym every day, teaching, and the door was open.

# Alma Ingle's Story

*I met Brendan in a jazz club. I was there with a friend and Brendan and this other fellow came over. It was the other fellow who did all the talking. We started going out and within a couple of weeks Brendan said, we'll get engaged. I thought it was a game. Looking back, I think Brendan wanted somewhere settled. He was living in digs and he wasn't happy. He missed his own family. I lived with my family on Newman Road. Our house was next door to where Brendan and I eventually settled. It was called Poplar Farm. There weren't any poplars, but in those days Wincobank was a village and we were surrounded by fields. My father was a coal merchant. It was a one-man, one-lorry business. He kept the coal in the farmyard.*

*I kept putting Brendan off and then I more or less said yes to keep him quiet, and I thought, if I change my mind it won't really matter. Then I thought, oh well there's nothing to lose, so I got married. Brendan wouldn't come home from the wedding reception because he was playing snooker. I came home on my own. That's been the story of my life – leaving him somewhere, talking usually, and coming home by myself.*

*He boxed for a club in the town and I went to watch him. I'd never seen boxing before but I thought he'd won. It looked one-sided to me but the other fellow got the decision. I was ringside and I stood up and started shouting at the referee. I was absolutely incensed that the other fellow had won. Brendan was so embarrassed he jumped out of the ring and started playing hell with me for showing him up. It was amateur boxing, and you don't behave like that at amateur boxing, Alma, everybody's a gentleman.*

*We bought a small terraced house but we were burgled and Brendan decided that was it: we should go to live in Dublin. We stayed with his family. Brendan's so much like his father it's unbelievable. His father was even more obsessed with his pigeons than Brendan is with his boxing. Brendan found a job, but I couldn't because I wasn't a Roman Catholic, basically. We were wasting our time over there so I came home, back to the farm, and discovered I was pregnant. Brendan was still over in Ireland and when I told him I was pregnant he said he'd come back after St Patrick's Day, which was six weeks away. I said, no, if you're not back this weekend don't bother coming. He came.*

*He used to give me his wages and he'd have his bus fare for work and a pound a week spending money. I had to manage on the rest. I said to Brendan, what are you giving me all your money for? and he said, well, I don't want the worry of having to manage on it. If it doesn't last to the end of the week, it's your problem, Alma, not mine. Brendan has always been hopeless with money. He still doesn't know how to take money out of a bank or how to write a cheque. If a letter comes with his name on it and it's got a window on the front, he'll not open it. I don't like the look of that, he'll say; you open it, Alma.*

*After the club started, I became involved in the boxing. The Amateur Boxing Association were short of judges in this area and Brendan said you'd better become a judge. I applied and the ABA tried to dissuade me. They didn't want woman judges. Eventually I persuaded them to let me take the course and then to let me take the exam. I said if I make a mess of the exam then fair enough, but I passed – came top as a matter of fact – against about a dozen fellows from South and West Yorkshire.*

*I started judging at a few shows but then two women down in Derbyshire applied to become judges and the ABA started panicking. What would happen if these women wanted to become referees? At that time, if you'd been judging for three years, you could apply to train as a referee. What would happen if a woman had to referee two heavyweights? they said. It was all so silly. I didn't want to be a referee, but the ABA decided the two women from Derbyshire couldn't pass out and they ended up banning all woman judges.*

*It didn't affect me because by that time our whole club was banned by the ABA. There was a complaint that pros and amateurs were training together in the gym, and they held an inquiry and banned the club, and Brendan. Brendan had no right of appeal because he was an ex-pro. He was devastated. He had one of his protests: he gave up drinking tea. It all seems farcical, now. We couldn't see what all the fuss was about. I think some people were jealous of Brendan's success.*

*Right from the beginning, Brendan produced champions. Peter Bennett was our first national schoolboy champion and Walter Clayton our first ABA junior champion. Then came Herol Graham, our first senior champion. I remember when we first met him. We borrowed a car to go over to a show at a miners' welfare club. Herol, who came from Nottingham, was there and he asked Brendan to take him on. He came back in the car with us and we put him in the same bedroom as two of our sons, John and Dominic. Herol stayed with us for three or four years before he found his own place. Everyone around the place thought he was wonderful, and they still do. But it was sad. He let Brendan down, and never reached his full potential. He should have been world champion, but he always picked the wrong sort of woman to hang around with, and he never really liked fighting. Naz was never away from the place, either. He was always with Brendan, talking boxing, living boxing, Brendan explaining what was happening with Herol and the other boxers. If Naz knew any of the pros were boxing, he'd be here straight from school and Brendan couldn't get away without him. He used to do all sorts to get Naz into the dinner shows. He'd keep him in the dressing room out of the way until everyone had had plenty to drink and wouldn't notice he was around.*

*Brendan puts up with a lot from his boxers that he wouldn't have taken from his own children. He idolises boxers. Anybody who gets in a ring has got to be courageous, and he's just in love with them all. He never expects people to let him down. He thinks if you're decent with people they'll never let you down, and he's always so surprised and hurt when they do. I could go over to the gym and weed ten of them out. I've said to Brendan, you're in for heartbreak again, get rid of them now before you spend too much time with them. And he says, I don't know how you can say that, Alma.*

*With Naz, everybody who knew him in the gym knew how he would turn out, what he'd be like if he made it in the big time – except Brendan. He'll never do a Herol Graham on me, Alma, he'd say, and I'd say well I hope he doesn't. Because he gets so hurt. He's devastated every time it happens.*

# CHAPTER SIX
## The Gentle Breeze

The same year that Brendan left Dublin, 1958, Salem Hamed, Naseem's father, began his own journey to Newman Road. It was more arduous and exotic than Brendan's. Sal was born in 1933 in the village of Malah, 120 miles north of the capital of the Yemen, Sana'a. His father, like his ancestors, was a farmer in a semi-desert area where little could be grown except for qat, a privet-like bush whose narcotic leaves are almost constantly chewed by 80 per cent of the male Yemeni population.

By the age of twelve, Sal was running his own small shop, travelling to Sana'a by donkey to buy stocks of sugar, tobacco and spices. As a young man, Sal, like many Yemenis, heard that work was to be had in the steel mills of Sheffield so he left his wife and home and travelled south to the British colony of Aden, from where he took a boat overladen with emigrants to Djibouti. From Djibouti, he went by boat to Madagascar and worked his way to Zanzibar, Nairobi and Mombasa where he boarded a ship heading for Marseilles via the Cape and West Africa. When he finally arrived in Sheffield, he worked in the steel mills, saving everything he could. In 1962 he was joined by his wife, Caira. They settled in Wincobank and a few years later bought a small general store, number 100, Newman Road. On 12 February 1974, Sal and Caira's fifth child, their third son, was born in the Northern General Hospital in Sheffield. He was named Naseem, which means Gentle Breeze.

Naseem stood in the corner of the ring in Brendan's gym, gloved up, ready to box, and made an announcement: 'Naseem Hamed, aged ten, flyweight, England and the Yemen.'

He bowed, stepped forward and dived into three forward somersaults across the canvas to the opposite corner, stood up, turned and did another three somersaults back. Across the other diagonal, Ryan Rhodes, aged eight, announced himself and also tumbled across the ring and back. 'Away you go,' said Brendan. They touched gloves and began to box.

The ritual was intended to help kids struck dumb by shyness. Announcing their names gave them a sense of identity. The somersaults, and front and back-flips when they were older, developed balance and an awareness of the space within the ropes, sprinkled them with stardust and built self-confidence. Brendan took the idea from a book. He was a painfully slow reader, making out the words one by one, but the books he read had a profound effect. *A Man Must Fight*, by Gene Tunney, was his favourite. Tunney, who won the world heavyweight title in 1926 when he beat Jack Dempsey, described his early days in New York. As a sixteen-year-old in 1914, he had come across a lightweight named Willie Green, who was both a professional actor and a boxer. Green was a young veteran who had fought 168 contests between the ages of seventeen and twenty-two. Watching Green sparring in a club in Greenwich Village, Tunney was deeply impressed: 'When he took the gloves off he threw a row of backflips. This advanced Green farther in my estimation. Here, I thought, was a great fighter, a great tumbler, a prominent actor, a person to be greatly admired.'

Brendan had great hopes for Naseem and Ryan Rhodes, two of the first he had taught from the beginning: they were his stars for the future, his first world champions, if Herol Graham didn't make it. Naseem was seven when he started, Ryan six. They became firm friends, tumbling, singing songs in the ring and fighting. Ryan lived a few miles away. His mother brought him to the gym after school and collected him later on. He didn't hang around Brendan's house like Naseem, so he never had the intensive education in boxing, religion, politics and life that Brendan gave Naseem. You might say Ryan was denied; or you might say he was spared.

Anyone who ever visited Brendan's gym and was trapped by his

Ancient Mariner eye and grabbed by the arm, knew some of Brendan's philosophy and sayings.

'Boxing is a wicked, dirty, horrible, rotten and vindictive game. It's the only sport where you can legally kill your opponent.'

'The only person who will ever lick you is yourself.'

'Don't drink, don't smoke, don't gamble, don't do drugs and don't chase women.'

'The biggest motivator in life is sex.'

'To be ignorant is sad. To be ignorant and not know you're ignorant is very sad. For you to know I'm ignorant and not help me, that's terrible.'

Every Sunday for nearly ten years, around six o'clock, winter and summer, rain and shine, Brendan and Naseem went for a walk. Brendan would start up Newman Road and call in at the shop for Naseem and they would go on together past Concord Park, up to Sheffield Lane Top, down Wood Bottom and back to Newman Road. It was about six miles round and it took them a little over two hours: two hours of talk.

It could have been an unequal partnership, the ten-year-old Arab boy and the middle-aged Irishman who had a theory and a story for every day of the year. It wasn't, because Naseem never entirely gave himself up to his teacher. Some of the kids worshipped Brendan. Ryan did. Naseem admired him and listened, but took Brendan's lessons *à la carte*. Naseem was always forward, cheeky, brazen. When Brendan gave him a nickname, 'the Arab' or 'the little Arab', Naseem gave him one back, 'Irish' or 'Old Irish'. There wasn't much point in calling Brendan Paddy or Old Paddy because that was how he referred to himself, sometimes going one step further: 'this thick old Paddy'.

By the time he turned eleven, Naseem was an expert boxer. He never lacked ego or courage. He had learned the steps and punches, the combinations. He had trained and sparred for years, mostly against older and bigger boys because among his peers only Ryan Rhodes could live with him. He had sparred against professionals, and had already begun to live the boxer's life. If Brendan was taking boxers to a show, Naseem always wanted to go. Whether it was in Liverpool or

Manchester, even London, Brendan would say, go and ask your mum, and Naseem would come back and say, yes, he could come along. Often they returned late at night. They'd bang on the door of the shop and wait in the car, sometimes for five minutes, until the door opened and Naseem nipped in.

In his schoolwork, Naseem was average and bored. He was small for his age, always the smallest in the class. He had pretty brown eyes and at first glance looked vulnerable. But his eyes held steady and his words were certain. When he was taunted, called 'Chocolate Drop' or 'Paki', he replied bluntly: 'I'm not Pakistani. I'm Arab, me.' And he was happy to fight. But no one wanted to fight him. After school, when he was supposed to go to Arabic classes, Naseem set off with his brothers, but at Brendan's gym near the bottom of the road, Naseem ducked inside.

When journalists and other visitors turned up at the gym, Brendan took them aside and pointed at Naseem, a tiny figure punching upwards at a punch-bag.

'He's the one, you know. He's going to be world champion.'

No one believed Brendan. He was always full of blarney, and anyway that kid was so small it was hard to believe he would ever be a real boxer.

Brendan would call Naseem over and introduce him.

'What are you going to be?'

Naseem would answer automatically, in a plain, matter-of-fact way, as if he was already tired of saying it, tired of the obvious.

'World champion.'

# CHAPTER SEVEN
## This Fellow Has It All

Brendan was getting ready to go out, fiddling with his bow-tie. He was always a bit embarrassed about wearing a dinner jacket. It wasn't his image. But he also liked to look smart. He justified it by calling it his hustling gear, because he used dinners and charity functions to extract promises of funds and favours for the club from local businessmen.

'Where are you off to?' asked his son, John.

'Down Cutler's Hall for a do.'

'Dinner show?'

'That's right.'

'Hold on a sec, I'll get Naz. Maybe he can get on as a spare.'

It was 24 February 1986, twelve days after Naseem's twelfth birthday. Under amateur boxing rules, boxers could take part in official contests when they were eleven. For championships, they also had to weigh a minimum of four and a half stone, and Naseem, at eleven, barely weighed four stone. He desperately wanted to box, to have a real fight so that he could show off in public what he could do in the gym. At school, during his year of frustration, everyone in his class had to give a demonstration of their hobby or interest. Next to the stamp collections, wood carvings and tricks with yo-yos, Naseem's display was stunningly original. He came into the classroom in his boxing gear, carrying a ghetto-blaster, turned it on and did five minutes' shadow boxing, full pace, every combination he knew and all the footwork, including the shuffle. Naseem's classmates were mighty impressed, but they didn't let on. They reckoned Naseem's head was big enough already, and they weren't going to swell it any further.

As Brendan finally tied his bow-tie, John was on the phone to Naseem, though they had only left each other ten minutes earlier.

'Finish your supper and come down quick,' said John. 'We're going to a show. And bring your gear.'

John was four years older than Naseem, but they knocked around together at Brendan's house and in the evenings would go up to the Pinegrove Country Club to play table tennis or pool. They sparred with each other for hour after hour. The gym was officially open morning and evening from Monday to Friday, and mornings only on Saturdays and Sundays. On Saturday afternoons, John and Naseem would have their own sessions. Sometimes they sparred, and sometimes John took Naseem on the pads. For Naseem, it was never hard work. It was play. While John pretended to be Sugar Ray Leonard or Marvin Hagler, Naseem was always himself – and he always had to win.

Grabbing his bag of gear, Naseem rushed down to Brendan's. He had been disappointed before, but maybe this time he would really get a fight. Brendan drove his Volkswagen minibus to the city centre with John and Naseem up front beside him, and parked round the back of the City Hall. They walked down to the Cutler's Hall, Brendan in his dinner jacket, John in a tracksuit, Naseem in his school clothes.

Cutler's Hall, built in 1832, is imposing and is meant to be. The cutlers of Sheffield were as proud, and had once been as wealthy, as any City of London livery company. Just inside the entrance, a grand staircase leads up to the banqueting chambers. At the top of the first broad flight of steps hangs a full-length portrait of the Queen, in oils. Brendan peeled off left up the stairs while John and Naseem went down to the basement where the boxers changed.

John knew the procedure well enough, for he looked after most of the amateurs in the gym when they boxed. He found the official in charge of the show and presented Naseem's medical card, which showed that he had been examined by a doctor, passed fit to box, but that he hadn't yet fought. 'Naseem Hamed, twelve years old,' John said. For a match to be made, there had to be an opponent within a year of Naseem's age and within four pounds of his weight. Naseem stood on the scales. Four stone, three pounds. Another boy, Pete

Ironmonger, weighed in at four stone six pounds. 'OK, that's a match,' said the official.

Most young boxers are nervous before their first bout. Some are scared to death. Naseem couldn't wait. This was his moment. In his boots and shorts, gloved up, he walked up the grand stairway and past the Queen. John walked with him, carrying a towel. The main banqueting chamber was a vast statement of grandiosity. On the walls hung portraits of Queen Victoria, the Duke of Wellington and assorted master cutlers. The ceiling, as high as a cathedral, was painted, and supported by marble pillars. Wall to wall around the chamber, tables were laid, each bought for the night by a local businessman to wine and dine his guests. But when Naseem walked through the double doors, he did not see the tables or pillars or paintings. His eyes were fixed on the structure right in the centre, under the biggest chandelier: the ring.

Dinner eaten, loyal toast drunk, cigars lit, waitresses back in the kitchens, the boxing commenced. Naseem climbed up the steps, ducked under the ropes and began to dance, bouncing on the canvas, holding his hands above his head like a belly dancer. No one had told him to do it. Naseem was just celebrating his arrival. The referee intercepted him. John Ingle heard him say to Naseem: 'Back to your corner, son.'

Ironmonger, Naseem's very first opponent, was taller, heavier and more experienced. He had had a few contests. But he didn't have a chance. Naseem had been boxing for nearly five years, training like a professional and with professionals. He had shared a ring with the most skilful boxer in Britain, Herol Graham. Already he had learned every punch and move.

At the first bell, Naseem took the perimeter of the ring, circling as Ironmonger plodded after him. Children who box usually flail at each other, fighting windmills, wincing with anxiety even as they attack. Many take their first punch on the nose and decide they don't like boxing after all. Some cry. Ironmonger was game enough, but he must have wished he was somewhere else. He couldn't land a punch. Naseem skipped into range, avoided Ironmonger's swings, landed a sharp combination of straight punches and was away, out of range. He repeated the process, with the same result, and just kept doing it. This was easy, this was boxing just like Brendan had always said. You make the other guy miss, and you hit him.

At the end of the first round, John dispensed the easiest advice of all. 'You're doing fine. Just keep on doing what you're doing.'

Naseem obliged. The second round was a repeat of the first; the third a repeat of the second. Naseem had won his first fight by a mile and the referee raised his arm.

Brendan watched the contest from a table by the door. He was a guest of Tom Wild, who owned an engineering firm and was a benefactor to the gym. For Brendan there were few surprises in Naseem's performance. He knew better than anyone, except maybe Naseem, how good he was. But one last question had been answered. Naseem could do it in public – do it when it wasn't practice or play, or against a sparring partner, but against an opponent when it mattered, in front of an audience. In fact, whereas most kids froze, gulping with nervousness, Naseem was completely at home, as brilliant, maybe more brilliant, than in the gym. And this was his first fight.

Because he had boxed as a spare, Naseem's name was not on the programme. But the top table awarded him the prize for the best boxer of the night, and Brendan, as Sheffield's leading boxing personality, the manager and trainer of Herol Graham, who three weeks earlier had won the European middleweight title, was called up to present the trophy.

Next morning, Naseem went straight to the pile of papers on the counter in the shop. The *Star*'s report of the charity boxing night at the Cutler's Hall led with an account of his bout. 'Look out Bomber Graham – the schoolboy terror is after you,' the paper said. Inevitably, it included a quote from Brendan: 'This fellow has it all. He's a natural.'

33

# CHAPTER EIGHT
## The Pity and the Waste

Brendan and Herol Graham were like father and son. Herol was eighteen and already one of the best amateur boxers in England when he left Nottingham to join Brendan, living in Sheffield as part of Brendan's family. Herol was a southpaw and Brendan taught him to box from the orthodox stance as well. Herol was always hard to hit. Brendan helped make him almost impossible to hit. He taught him to switch-hit, to box square on and from the side. He taught him all the counters. He taught him the steps and how to train, how to keep his weight right. He took a brilliant boxer and made him better. He tried to make him believe in himself. He gave Herol the usual advice: that the only person who could beat him was himself, and that he shouldn't smoke, drink, gamble, do drugs or chase women; and when he knew him better he especially told him that he shouldn't chase women.

They were inseparable. Together, Herol and Brendan won the Amateur Boxing Association middleweight title in 1978. Herol turned professional with Brendan as his manager and together they won the British, Commonwealth and European titles at light-middleweight and the British and European titles at middleweight. But it was more than that. They shared a dream, and a fight against adversity. The dream was to win a world title and the fight was the political and financial struggle to get the chance. Herol fought whoever was put in front of him. He'd done that more than thirty times and had always won. Brendan had negotiated the matches that took Herol to European championship level, and he had done it without giving up contractual control. But for a boxer of Herol's talent, the purses had been too small, the television too infrequent, the following limited to Sheffield, and the profile far too low. Brendan and Alma had even mounted promotions themselves, once putting their house on the line to borrow the money to stage an open-air show at Bramall Lane, Sheffield United's football ground.

Herol, unfortunately, was in what promoters called the who-needs-him club. If a promoter had a fighter who was a good ticket-seller, he kept him away from Herol, because Herol was bound to win. And then the promoter wouldn't know what to do with Herol. He was the boxer who couldn't be hit, the defensive master, but people who went to boxing didn't go to admire the art. They wanted the thrill of the knockout and the slugging match to oblivion. Herol had the wrong image. He seemed vulnerable, unsure of himself, and his voice was high-pitched. He was more like a gymnast or a dancer than a boxer. So he was labelled as bad box-office.

But despite all that, Brendan and Herol had almost done it. Even the best-connected boxers found it difficult to avoid him for ever as he climbed the British and European rankings until his claims to challenge for those titles could not be denied. At number four in the world rankings, Herol could no longer be overlooked.

And then, on the threshold, they split up. It was all about money, so it was said. Brendan sold his management contract with Herol, which had three years to run, to Barney Eastwood, the Belfast bookmaker, for £75,000. Brendan was to be kept on as trainer, but he had given up his right to manage Herol. He had broken the partnership.

Brendan said he wanted financial security, a return for the nine years' work he had put into developing Herol. It seemed he was admitting defeat, admitting that without the right connections, without selling out, he would never get Herol even a shot at the world title. Brendan tried to argue that it would be better for Herol. Brendan would still be training him and Barney Eastwood, who managed and promoted Barry McGuigan, the world featherweight champion, would be able to open the doors to a world title.

At first Herol accepted it, although he must have been hurt. But then he became resentful. He told Brendan he wanted £25,000, a third of the sum Barney Eastwood had paid Brendan. Herol said that he and Brendan had always promised each other that when the big money came along, they would share it. Initially, Brendan refused: the

£75,000 was his money, his pension. But an agreement was sorted out whereby Brendan would pay Herol the £25,000 in instalments, deducted from his fees as trainer. But that never happened, because Herol walked out of Brendan's gym.

The split wasn't all about money. Brendan had a grievance which he kept secret. He has never said what it was, but it shattered their relationship. All that is known is that Brendan felt so strongly about it at the time that he wanted to kill Herol. He even planned how to do it. He was going to slip an iron bar up his sleeve and take it into the gym while Herol was sparring. When Herol came back to the corner at the end of a round, for a word of advice or a dab with a towel, Brendan was going to smash his skull. It was a terrible way to kill someone, but symbolic. The boxer fights for his life in the ring and his only haven is the corner. To find a mortal enemy there is to be killed by the parent, in the nest.

Brendan retained enough reason to play the film a little further. Herol struck dead on the canvas, his brains spilt; sparring partner in shock; the kids around the gym quiet, uncomprehending; the police arriving; Brendan led away, never to return.

Brendan did not kill Herol.

A month after Brendan and Herol had split up, Herol defended his European middleweight title against Sambu Kalambay, a dangerous and experienced fighter, in London. Herol trained not in Sheffield but in Belfast, not with Brendan but with Eddie Shaw, Barry McGuigan's trainer, and Frederico Plummer, a Panamanian trainer brought in by Barney Eastwood. Plummer told the press he was working on sorting out Herol's defence.

For the first time in nine years, Herol fought without Brendan in the corner. And for the first time, after thirty-eight professional fights, he lost. Brendan and Alma were among the spectators at the Wembley Arena. However strongly Brendan felt about whatever Herol had done, he didn't want to see him licked. As Herol was beaten to a standstill late in the fight, failing to move, getting seriously hurt for the first time in his life, Brendan was torn inside for the pity of it, and the waste.

# CHAPTER NINE

## The Fly Came to the Web

Naseem hated to lose, whether it was at snooker, cards or staying the longest under water. Most of all, he hated to lose at boxing. In sixty-seven amateur contests, he lost five times. All five losses were by decision of the judges, and all five, according to Brendan and Naseem, were daylight robbery. The blazered officials, some of whom had been instrumental in getting Brendan and the St Thomas's club banned from amateur boxing, made no secret of their distaste for Naseem. Instead of wearing a plain colour, such as blue or white, he arrived in a gold gown. Instead of slipping under the ropes, he vaulted them. Instead of holding his hands up at all times in the posture of a guardsman, he let them dangle at his sides in the manner of Muhammad Ali. Instead of showing respect, he stuck out his tongue. Instead of exhibiting concern for a fallen opponent, he celebrated with flips and somersaults.

Amateur boxing officials were always at pains to keep at bay the circus trappings of the professional game. After one tumbling routine, a referee told Naseem: 'If you ever do that again, I'll sling you out.' Another time, Naseem dangled his hands and was given a standing count, as if he had been knocked down, because the referee, Gordon Ibinson, ruled that he wasn't defending himself. Ibinson, a stickler for the letter of the rules, was a persistent thorn in Brendan's flesh. During a single session of the North-East divisonal championships, Ibinson disqualified three boxers from Brendan's gym for offences that were merely stylistic. Brendan believed that Ibinson was one of those responsible for getting him banned from amateur boxing. Some six years later, Naseem and Brendan would come across Ibinson again and would exact the sweetest retribution.

When Naseem suffered his fifth and last defeat as an amateur, against Dean Pithie in a junior ABA semi-final in Manchester in May 1989, Brendan and Naseem decided enough was enough. If the judges were going to ignore the evidence, matters had to be taken out of their hands. 'From now on,' Brendan said, 'I'll set you a different routine in the gym and you're going to start knocking them out.'

It seemed a logical progression, but it entailed a loss of innocence, an acceptance of the impurity of boxing. Naseem had long wanted to be able to punch harder. He knew it would confer on him power, physical and abstract. He wanted the acknowledgement from the man opposite, be he opponent, sparring partner, even brother, that he was his physical master. When you outsmarted a man, made him miss and cuffed him, he could laugh it off. But if you won the trick and hurt him, you were better.

For Brendan, skill was the ideal. Boxing should be a test of applied technique, not of crude power. Surely that was why there were judges at ringside, assessing the comparative merits of the boxers, noting the blows landed by each man. By having such an examination, boxing was able to appear technical, civilised, a once-bloody sport made acceptable, like fencing. The reality was very different. Judges could be stupid or corrupt. You could only rely on them to be unreliable, unless they were deliberately biased, for amateur boxing was riddled with feuds and jealousies. The only way to be certain of victory was to knock your opponent out or so hurt him that the referee was forced to stop the fight. There was another consideration, which Brendan knew would apply once Naseem turned professional. Followers of boxing, and those who promote and publicise it, invariably pay lip service to the art and science of the sport. But it is big punching, and above all the symbolic execution of the knockout, that most excites.

There were dangers in giving Naseem the key to the armoury, Brendan knew that. Power encourages the bully in a boxer, it gives him a sense of omnipotence, makes him want to measure his power against the other man's by taking a punch as well as giving one. It encourages in him a multitude of vices, including short cuts in training, because stamina and speed seem unnecessary, and the neglect of defence.

Reluctantly, but of necessity, Brendan taught Naseem to bang, to turn the sweetness of his timing to explosive use. Naseem made greater use of the heavy corn-filled punch-bag, learning to time shots so that it swung violently on its chain, and his work on the pads, always fast and accurate, became sharper and more spiteful. He learned to plant his feet and turn his hips from a solid base, to tap the strength of his legs, upper body, arm and wrist and bring it all to bear at once in the propulsion of the gloved fist. The idea was not to punch at an opponent to score, but to drive right through him, to be accelerating at the point of impact.

Some boxers enjoy natural power, a big punch. Some learn it. But almost all can deliver it only as a single blow, usually with their favoured hand and only in circumstances in which the opponent, the target, is perfectly placed. Henry Cooper knocking down Muhammad Ali, for example. Very few master the trick of delivering power in combinations of punches, from different angles and with either hand. Naseem managed it because when he added power there was no sacrifice. The speed and mesmerising combinations remained. He had the same delivery system with a much more deadly arsenal. Once Naseem started punching hard, he knew he was going to win, every time he boxed.

In 1990 Naseem was selected to box for Young England against the US junior Olympic team. Naseem, John Ingle and Kieran McGrath, a pal of Brendan's who did a great deal of work for the club, drove in Kieran's van to the Heathrow Park Hotel, where the match was held. The Young England team comprised the national schoolboy champions at every weight. Most of them were members of the big amateur boxing clubs in east London such as Repton and West Ham. It seemed like a reunion for the officials, coaches and boxers from London, and Naseem, John and Kieran felt out of place. They left the others and went upstairs to the single room Naseem had been allocated to rest for the afternoon. Naseem sat on the bed, John on the floor and Kieran against a wall.

Later, there was a bang on the door. Kieran opened it. It was one of the Young England coaches, and he wasn't happy.

39

'What the hell are you doing? It's five past six. You should have been down at six sharp for the team talk.'

'No one told us,' said John.

'It's on your agenda.'

'No one gave us an agenda.'

'Hold on, hold on,' Kieran said. 'Naseem's been praying. He has to pray five times a day and one of the times is six o'clock. Show some respect for the lad's religion.'

'Oh, right, sorry. I didn't realise.'

When Naseem arrived in the dressing room, he was met by a row of gloomy faces. Straight away he could tell that most of the lads lined up on the benches thought they were going to lose. Given the comparative strength of amateur boxing in Britain and the United States, such pessimism was not unreasonable.

'What's up with you lot?' said Naseem. 'Why don't you smile and relax instead of looking like you're going to get beat?'

But Naseem's were wasted words. One by one, they were called to box, made their way to the ring like the condemned, and returned battered and beaten. Nine went out and nine lost. Naseem was the tenth.

As Naseem, wearing his gold gown, stood by the door to the arena, ready to go on, the chief national coach stopped him and pointed at the gown.

'You're boxing for England,' he said. 'You're not here to represent yourself, but to represent your country, got it? Now take that off.'

Naseem had been confident, determined. Now he was angry. Here he was, about to box for England, and they were knocking him back. There was no way he was going to lose, even if his opponent, Danny Acevedo, a Puerto Rican, was highly rated. He was definitely going to win. He was going to do to Acevedo what the other Americans had been doing to the Young England team.

For once, Naseem decided not to argue. He gave the coach a blank stare, removed the gold gown and walked to the ring without it. But he took the rest of his show with him. He jumped into the ring and did a front flip across the canvas, getting a cheer from the crowd. When the

Dublin days: Brendan (*left*) ready to rumble on his First Communion day, 22 June 1947, with his three sisters and brother Peter

To love and to cherish (but wait until I've finished playing snooker): Brendan and Alma outside St Thomas's Church, Wincobank, on their wedding day, 5 August 1961

Put up your dukes: Brendan and Billy Hall, square up in the early
1970s with Frank Middleton and Steve Stocks watching

(*Facing page, above*) Fight factory: Brendan inside the St Thomas's gym
(*Below*) The first great partnership, before the first great split:
Brendan takes Herol Graham on the pads

Team St Thomas's: Naseem (*centre*) with, among others, his brother Nabeel, Herol Graham and Brendan

Precocious prince: Naseem with Nabeel, John Ingle
and big Dermot Gascoyne

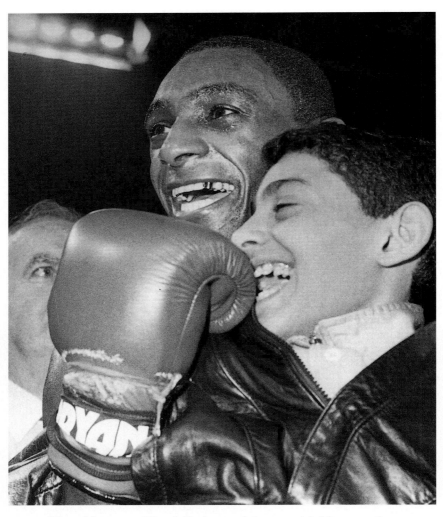

The old master: Herol Graham celebrates with Naseem after
Herol's victory over Charlie Boston in Belfast

Johnny Nelson with his Lonsdale belt: his amazing career
ran from humiliation to triumph

Best Wishes
N. Hamed

Manager - Brendan Ingle
0742 423392

Postcard for a prince

bell rang, he planted three quick hurtful shots and moved away, switching, hitting off the wrong foot, the shuffle, the combinations, the lead with the uppercut, every trick he knew, and with power. What did the England coach, who was in the corner, tell Naseem between rounds? Probably to stop showing off, to watch out and keep up his guard. In any case, Naseem wasn't listening. He was too busy thrashing Acevedo, whose sole achievement was to survive. After three virtuoso rounds, Naseem didn't bother to wait for the judges' decision. He did a cartwheel and a somersault to celebrate his victory.

When the match was over, some businessmen in the crowd, who had come to cheer for England and had to wait until Naseem arrived with his fireworks, pressed money on him. Naseem went back to Sheffield in Kieran's van with £200.

That year, 1990, Naseem, at sixteen, won the first of his two junior ABA titles, in the light-flyweight division. In the final at the York Hall in Bethnal Green, east London, he fought a lad from Kent called Michael Wright. Naseem had problems. He hurt his right hand early in the fight and had to keep out of trouble, stay out of range. The crowd, with the hall and the balcony packed like a cockpit, started to scream for Wright, their man, to punish Naseem. 'He's only a dancer. Get the black bastard!'

Naseem stepped up the pace, and began to punch, using the right hand as well as the left, ignoring the pain. He won on points and was booed from the ring, and booed again later when he went forward to collect his trophy for winning the title.

Afterwards, Brendan and Naseem were in a café across the road. Naseem had a beefburger and chips.

'Enjoying your food?' said Brendan.

'Yeah.'

'You know your mate Nigel's in the nick, don't you?'

'Yeah, so what?'

'I wonder if he's enjoying his porridge as much as you and me are enjoying this?'

'That's a horrible thing to say.'

'That's right. Now, listen. When there's been an IRA bomb, people say to me, you Irish bastards. And I say to them, get it right, thick Irish bastards, and I walk away. Dealing with idiots. Naz, you'll have a chance to make millions. All you've got to do is smile, shake hands, be nice and close your ears. And then get in the ring and get paid for beating people up.'

Brendan knew Naseem was angry that he had been insulted, but if he thought he was upset, he was wrong. For where Brendan tended to avoid confrontation, to try to understand and defuse hostility, Naseem thrived on hatred and fed on it. The more the crowd wanted him to lose, the better, and the more viciously, he fought.

Brendan had a telephone call from Wilf Swindles, the trainer of Mark Epton, a professional flyweight, with impeccable credentials. Epton came from Mexborough, near Doncaster. He had been the British amateur champion three times and England team captain. He had turned professional, had won six fights out of six, and was preparing to challenge the British and European flyweight champion, Pat Clinton. Epton would get a purse of £18,000.

'Could Mark spar with your lad, Hamed?' Swindles enquired.

On the face of it, it was a crazy, dangerous proposition: to ask Naseem, a sixteen-year-old amateur, to box a top-class professional in full training for a European title fight.

'Sure,' said Brendan. 'Come on over.'

The gym was busy a few days later when Swindles and Epton came in, Epton carrying his gear in a huge bag. Brendan was up by the ring, but he spotted them straight away. The fly had come to the web. Naseem had already trained that evening. He'd done an hour's sparring, flat out, knocking spots off everyone. So he only did three rounds with Epton. But he had the better of it, not just surprising Epton, but hurting him. Epton put on a brave face and did some work on the punch-bags before getting changed. But Swindles wasn't going to leave it at that.

'Thanks very much. Could we come back tomorrow night and maybe we could do six rounds?'

'Sure,' said Brendan. 'No problem.'

When Swindles and Epton were out of the door, Brendan grabbed Naseem. 'Epton's coming back tomorrow. He's going to try to slaughter you.'

'Good.'

By the next evening, Brendan had rigged up a video camera, and the ring was surrounded by the regulars. Even with headguards and heavy sparring gloves, it would be a real fight, a test of Naseem.

All eyes were on the ring as the buzzer sounded and away they went. Naseem, never one to wait, attacked from the first. He hurt Epton to the body, opened a cut near his eye, despite the headguard, split his nose, bashed him up, did a job on him. Epton was a proud man. He wouldn't give in. He took his beating for six rounds.

When it was over, Brendan towelled down Naseem and unlaced his gloves. 'You've finished his career. He won't box again.'

Epton took his bruises into the shower. When he came out, he admitted to John Ingle that it was all over for him. If he couldn't beat a kid of sixteen, then what was the point? He didn't box Pat Clinton for the European title. He wasn't paid £18,000. Still unbeaten as a professional, he retired from boxing.

# CHAPTER TEN

## The Last Adjustment

After their fall-out and the awful loss to Sumbu Kalambay, there had been a partial reconciliation between Herol Graham and Brendan. And now Naseem, along with Ryan Rhodes, crouched at the bottom of the steps in the corner of the ring in which Herol was making his second attempt to win the world middleweight title. Further up the steps, leaning their elbows on the canvas, were Brendan and John Ingle, Herol's seconds.

The fight, against Julian Jackson on 24 November 1990, was in a cavernous cabaret lounge in a casino in Marbella on the Costa del Sol in Spain. It was an unlikely venue for a boxer from Britain and one from the Virgin Islands, but maybe it was appropriate for what looked like Herol's last throw of the dice.

To be present on such occasions was all part of Naseem's education, and there was never a better-educated young fighter than Naseem. Long before he turned professional, he knew the ropes. He rubbed shoulders with Herol and the others as they trained for important contests, saw the physical work, the making weight, the sparring, the tapering off before the fight. He noted the ones who took short cuts, or couldn't concentrate because of worries unconnected with their fighting, and he saw what happened to them. And if Naseem didn't see the point, Brendan told him. 'See him, he missed training three days this week, he's fighting next Saturday and he's thinking about his girlfriend who's left him, and if he doesn't get his head right he'll get beat.'

For years, Naseem had been taken by Brendan to boxing shows at every level, from amateur nights in working men's clubs to world championships. He had seen it all: the nerves of the dressing room; the false bravado that evaporated into dread; the good cornermen who watched carefully and spoke softly between rounds, and the ones who screamed and spread panic; the referees who posed in monogrammed shirts; the managers whose boxers always lost; the boxers who looked tough and the ones who were; the old pros who knew how to survive, the young toughs who led with their chins; above all, the boxers who were beaten inside their own heads before the first bell.

Naseem would come to believe he had been chosen by God. But it was equally true that he had chosen himself and had been chosen by Brendan. From almost the very beginning, they both knew he could go to the summit, and prepared for it. That was why they walked and talked together every Sunday evening, and why, whenever someone from the gym fought for a title, home or abroad, Naseem was there.

Naseem watched as Herol fought Julian Jackson in the casino in Marbella, and Herol was winning easily, skating it. This was Herol at his best, moving, slipping, sticking his man with the jab. This time, surely, Herol was finally going to win the world title. After Herol returned to the gym in Newman Road and Brendan agreed to train him again, Herol had notched up three comeback victories and in 1989 at last had a shot at the world title, taking on Mike McCallum of Jamaica, one of the most formidable fighters in the world at any weight, at the Albert Hall in London. Herol lost on a split points decision. If the referee had not deducted a point for holding, after Herol had turned McCallum on the ropes like a matador slipping a bull, a manoeuvre that usually draws applause from the knowing ones at ringside, Herol would have won. It was another sad, wasted night. But for Naseem, who that night had the job of guarding the dressing-room door, there was a lesson that wasn't wasted: world titles have to be ripped from the hands of the holder, not left to the judges' scorecards.

Herol's last chance was to beat Jackson in Marbella. It was a great chance, too, for as a boxer Jackson was nowhere near Herol's class. In fact, Jackson had but one recommendation: the best knockout punch in the world. That was a dangerous calling card, but it seemed irrelevant because Herol was boxing Jackson to pieces, and the sense of expectation among the group squatting beneath Herol's corner was rising. Jackson was not just being outclassed, he was getting busted up. He had been cut around the eye and it couldn't go on much longer.

Naseem was more than an observer. He had been Herol's chief sparring partner, both in Sheffield and in a training camp in Spain for the last eight days before the fight. It was highly unusual, even irregular, for a sixteen-year-old amateur to help a professional prepare for a world title fight, especially at several divisions above his own weight, but there was sense in it. Naseem, who was already as outstanding as Herol in movement and skill, was the perfect foil to sharpen Herol's speed and defence. For everyone knew what was required for Herol to win: box at range and avoid Jackson's sucker punch.

From the ringside steps, Naseem gazed up into the TV lights, watching Herol do as he please, a typical Herol exhibition. Jackson couldn't lay a glove on him, and soon the cut eye was almost closed.

Just before the end of the third round, Herol was a little careless and Jackson had his first success, catching Herol flat on the mouth. It didn't seem important, because as Herol made for his corner, the referee had a hard look at Jackson's eye and thought about stopping the fight. Instead, he decided to give Jackson one more round.

Herol sat on his stool and Brendan, as usual, pulled out his gumshield. Jackson had caught him, and he could punch, all right. Several of Herol's teeth were embedded in the gumshield. Years before, Herol had worn a denture for his front teeth, but his girlfriend at the time had teased him about it and he had decided to have a bridge fitted. It cost more than £2,000. The bridge had broken off into the gumshield and Brendan was holding the whole ensemble in his hand, wondering what to do with it.

'Don't take 'em out. Just leave them in,' Herol said.

Brendan carefully replaced the gumshield, with the teeth, in Herol's mouth.

'You're winning easy,' Brendan said. 'You've closed his eye and they'll stop the fight soon. Just keep him on the back foot, hit and get out of the way. Keep moving.'

But Brendan could tell that Herol wasn't listening, that Herol was angry, that Herol was thinking: that bastard's broke my bridge and I'm going to make him pay, I'm going to get rid of him.

In the fourth round, Herol, against all his instincts, against everything he had ever done in the ring, went looking for a fight. He moved forward, ready to unload, looking for Jackson. And he never saw it. But then hardly anyone saw it. John Ingle said it was as if a man on the balcony had shot Herol through the brain with a high-powered rifle. That was the effect, but what happened was simple enough: Herol walked on to a right-hand punch and was out cold before he hit the canvas, face first.

In that moment, Brendan knew for sure what he had always feared: that Herol would never win a world title. And it wasn't just bad luck. Nor was it vanity, and nor was it because some girlfriend had teased him years ago. There was something missing. And Brendan began to suspect that there might be something missing in himself, that he might never take a boxer to a world title.

In the dressing room, Herol, who had recovered his senses, was trying to make light of his defeat. Just one of those things. Unlucky. Ryan Rhodes was crying. Another of Brendan's professionals who had made the trip, the loyal and popular Johnny Nelson, was remembering that when he had been house-sitting with Herol in the weeks before the fight Herol, had put on videos of Jackson's fights, but hadn't bothered to watch beyond the first minute or so. Perhaps he preferred not to see what Jackson's punches could do to a man, but surely he should have studied him better. Naseem stood on his own, trying not to cry, absorbing another lesson, and a painful one.

It was a time of great frustration. Herol had blown his chances of a world title, and so, too, had Johnny Nelson, a cruiserweight who was much less naturally gifted than Herol, but who had somehow struggled up to championship class only to freeze on the big occasion.

Naseem's main problem was getting fights. In 1991, his last year as an amateur, he was still too young to take part in the senior ABA championships. He won another junior championship and a boys' club title, but in open competition no one would take him on. They hadn't for almost three years. He was too dangerous.

After leaving school with two GCSE passes, in English (grade F) and painting and drawing (grade G), Naseem had a part-time job as a trainee telephone engineer, a job set up for him by Brendan. But he was really a full-time amateur boxer. Naseem only took the work because he was given so much time off that he could train when he wanted, and because he needed the money. The idea that he might find it useful to have a trade in case he didn't make it as a boxer was ridiculous.

A phone call that John Ingle took one evening in October 1991 led to Naseem's last amateur fight. The call came from the trainer and matchmaker at the Ancoats and Miles Platting Lads Boxing Club in Manchester, a club on the edge of Moss Side, which had the reputation of being the most violent neighbourhood in Britain, one of the few where gunfire was regularly heard at night.

'We've got a big show coming up at the club,' the trainer said. 'There's an Irish team coming over to box us. It's sold out, but we've got a problem. There's no one to fight Brodie.'

Now that would be a problem, John thought. Michael Brodie was their star turn, as big in Manchester as Naseem was in Sheffield, and he had won five national titles. He was a tough nut who stopped most of his opponents. Most of the locals who had bought tickets would have done so to see Brodie, and it wouldn't be too clever if he didn't box.

'Who do you want?' John said casually, knowing the answer.

'Naz.'

'Isn't Brodie too light for Naz?'

'He's seven stone, ten pounds, just weighed him.'

'Well Naz is eight stone two, so he's too heavy.'

'Can't you get Naz under eight stone?'

'I can ask him,' John said.

John knew that Naseem would be determined to fight Brodie and so he was. He hadn't fought in months, and Brodie had a big reputation. Naseem wanted it badly, even if it meant having to take off weight.

'Naz'll take it,' John said when he phoned back the Manchester trainer.

'Just make sure he's under eight stone,' the trainer said.

It was a rough night when John and Naseem crossed the Pennines by the Woodhead Pass. They were driven to Manchester by Jimmy Wood, an intense, gnarled man in his fifties, who had an alarming habit of grabbing people and staring in their faces when he spoke to them. Jimmy Wood was a moneylender who claimed to be 'a quarter-millionaire'. Every afternoon, he worked out in Brendan's gym, sweating profusely as he swung alternate hands at the heavy bag. The journey was light-hearted, all three laughing and joking, for an impending contest, even against someone as hard as Brodie on his home turf, was not a worry for Naseem or those around him. Negative thoughts never intruded.

At the venue, the hall of a working men's club that could accommodate several hundred people, Naseem weighed in straight away: seven stone, thirteen pounds. Then Brodie weighed in: eight stone, one pound. Rightly or wrongly Naseem and John felt done. They went to find Brodie's trainer.

'You made me get down in weight. You made me starve myself,' Naseem said. 'We know when we've been set up.'

But an edge of anger never hurt Naseem when he came to fight. In the dressing room, which all the boxers shared, he smiled when Brodie, sitting on a bench, gave him the evil eye.

The hall was full to bursting and the crowd well fuelled and boisterous. It was a big show. Brodie against Naseem, both aged seventeen, the two best young boxers in the north of England, maybe all England, was naturally top of the bill. Naseem had left behind his gold gown in favour of a new image. He wore a Mexican poncho. When he climbed into the ring, for once not bothering to vault the ropes, Brodie's family and friends were booing and whistling. There were shouts of 'Dirty, flash, black bastard!' around the hall. Brodie himself arrived to prolonged cheers. It was several hundred of Manchester against three of Sheffield.

The noise grew to uproar as the first bell sounded, the crowd urging

Brodie to victory on a wave of noise. Naseem circled for a few seconds before moving into range. As he did so, Brodie adjusted his headguard, a mandatory protection for amateurs. It was a habit of Brodie's. Some boxers hitch up their trunks, others bang their gloves together or bite on their gumshield. Brodie liked to adjust his headguard with his gloves, so that it felt just right. As he did so, Naseem struck twice, left, right, straight through the middle. Brodie pitched forward on to his hands and knees. Silence. Brodie stayed kneeling, shaking his head slowly in disbelief. He began to get up, but too late. He was counted out. The master of ceremonies consulted the timekeeper and announced the result. Jimmy Wood made a note on the cover of his programme, which he took home and kept safe. The fight, including the count to ten, had lasted thirty-two seconds.

# Johnny Nelson's Story

*When I was a kid in the 1970s, I had no love for boxing, but my hero was Muhammad Ali. He said a lot of things young black guys like me wanted to say but didn't have the bottle. He was the voice for a lot of people. I had an older brother called Alan. I suppose I worshipped him. I used to follow him all over the place when he let me. He was a boxer and he used to go to Brendan's gym with his friends and then come back and sit in the dining room, talking about boxing, laughing and joking. I couldn't join in because I knew nothing about boxing.*

*So I decided to box, but Alan said start somewhere else and then maybe later on you can come down to our gym. He'd walk out of the house and go down to Brendan's gym, and I'd go off in the other direction to another gym. Except that I didn't go. I used to hide behind the wall until Alan was out of sight and go back into the house. He'd come home about six o'clock and I'd make out I'd been in the other gym. That went on for about a year.*

*Eventually, it must have been about 1980, I said to Alan, let me come down to Brendan's gym and he said, all right then. For two years, we used to go to the gym, but once we got off the bus at the bottom of Newman Road, we* didn't know each other. No one knew we were related and Alan beat me up in sparring more than anyone else.

One day Brendan came round to our house to see Alan, who had turned professional by then, and I was sat there watching television, and Brendan said, hey Johnny, what are you doing here? I said, I live here. Brendan looked at Alan and then looked at me and he asked us, are you two brothers? and I said yeah, and Brendan started laughing.

When I boxed as an amateur, I won three fights out of fifteen. In the gym, I could hear people laughing when I used to spar. I heard them say, this kid's crap. Brendan said, I think your style might be more suited to being a professional. He said I wouldn't get hurt and I might achieve something, but it would take a lot of digging to find it. He said I would make some money but it would be win, lose and draw for me. I turned pro and lost my first three fights and I thought, if I get to five fights and I haven't won one, I'm jacking it in. Brendan told me I was very young mentally. You get guys like Naseem and Ryan Rhodes who in the ring had the mentality of thirty-year-olds when they were nineteen. Outside the ring, they had the mentality of nineteen-year-olds. But I was immature in and out of the ring.

I won a few and lost a couple and then came the Crawford Ashley fight. They were building him up as something special, so they put me in to get knocked out. Before I got in the ring against Ashley, Brendan said, Johnny, I want you to flip over the rope. I thought, God, how embarrassing. Johnny, Brendan said, I want you to flip over the rope and when they introduce you to the crowd, I want you to shout your name, do a back-flip, put your hands in the air and do an Ali-shuffle. I pleaded but Brendan said, you just do it, it'll send his cornerman mad and it'll do his head in. So I did it, and then I stood there staring at Ashley and he shuffled away and his cornerman said, stand away, don't let him disturb you, keep cool. Brendan said, keep on top of him. I kept the pressure on all the time and I beat him.

I won my next six fights and in 1990 I had my first world title chance, against Carlos de Leon, in Sheffield. I had a dream a week before the fight. The referee had both our hands up after the fight, and de Leon was looking across at me, smiling, and a man in a pinstripe suit was walking out of the hall. I told Brendan about the dream and he said, just ignore it. I did everything right in training and I thought, I can do this, I can do this. I knew

51

*that the people in the gym were my family and that if I looked bad it would make my family look bad. But as soon as I got out there and I saw all the famous people at ringside, the pressure was on and I just froze. That was when the boy came out and not the man. I just didn't fight. Brendan tried everything, pleading, shouting, he slapped me, but it was no use.*

*It was a draw and de Leon kept the title, and a lot of spectators walked out. A few days later, Brendan and I were in the car, and we stopped at some roadworks and one of the workmen banged on the window and shouted, Nelson, Ingle, we want our money back! I was depressed and if it hadn't been for Brendan talking to me constantly, I would never have got over it.*

*Two years later I got another chance for a world title when I fought James Warring in Fredericksburg, Virginia. I kept saying to myself, I must redeem myself, make sure it doesn't happen again, and I went out of the corner and someone shouted out, Remember the de Leon fight! James, get after him boy! and all my doubts came back, and I froze again and lost on points.*

*Brendan told me I was dead commercially in England, I would have to fight all over the world, in everyone else's backyard, and I made a living sparring and fighting everywhere from East Germany to New Zealand. In Sheffield, I was still living at home, a real mummy's boy, and Brendan said, you've got to move out and mature, start being a man. So I moved out when I was twenty-six, and started paying my own bills and growing up. I got married and we had a baby, and it all made me more positive about my life and my career.*

*Early in 1997 I was asked to go over to France as a sparring partner for Patrice Aoussi, who was training to defend his European cruiserweight title against Terry Dunstan. Brendan said, just do enough to hold your own, don't show him what you can do, because you might be fighting him one day. I spent a week there and I was tempted to let my punches go because he was very arrogant and was bullying people in the gym, but I took it easy and came home. Then one Thursday Brendan said, do you want to box for the European title? and I said, yeah, when's the fight? and he said, Saturday, Dunstan's pulled out and you've got the fight if you want it. I went out to France again and Aoussi had this smirk on his face, like he's just got a sparring partner to beat up for the European title. I let him think that, keeping very quiet, with my head down, acting like a loser right up to the fight. But when I got in the ring, I stood up straight with a big smile on my face and I could see he was thinking, who's this guy? but there was no turning back, I showed him what I can really do and I won the title.*

*Brendan has been very patient with me, like a father with his own child. He's been very forgiving because I've brought more disgrace to the gym than anybody because of my performances against de Leon and Warring. It's my job to redeem the gym. When I win the world title, the people who saw the de Leon fight and the Warring fight will say, what's Brendan Ingle done to him? Then I'll be redeemed because Brendan will get the credit he deserves.*

# CHAPTER ELEVEN

## The Princely Professional

Brendan held a loud-hailer to his mouth. 'Come and see the Arabian Knight, Prince Naseem Hamed, the greatest boxer since Muhammad Ali, the greatest thing since sliced bread! The Prince makes his début tonight, eight o'clock in the leisure centre. Come and see the Prince!'

The shoppers in the pedestrian precinct in the centre of Mansfield stood and stared. Naseem, standing beside Brendan in Arab costume, a shawl and headdress, and carrying a ceremonial dagger, was acutely embarrassed, a rare feeling for him.

On 14 April 1992, six months after disposing of Michael Brodie in his last amateur fight, Naseem had his first fight as a professional, being paid £1,000 to take on Ricky Beard of Dagenham.

In many respects, nothing had changed. For years, Naseem had been a professional in every way, save income. And Brendan had been singing his praises far and wide, though not in Mansfield's shopping centre. But now he was more than Naseem's teacher and father figure. He was Naseem's manager – and that meant selling him.

First came the name. Brendan had a way with names. He once had a black West Indian boxer called Fidel Castro Smith (his father was an ardent communist). There were many black fighters in British boxing, but few black people who went to the fights, so Brendan changed Fidel Smith's ring name to Slugger O'Toole. O'Toole was kitted out in emerald green with a shamrock on his boxing trunks and Brendan made sure all his Irish friends in Sheffield bought tickets for his first appearance. 'He's not Irish, he's black,' they shouted at Brendan, who was in O'Toole's corner. 'Who says you can't have a black Irishman?' Brendan shouted back. It was certainly confusing, because at one time both Fidel Castro Smith and Slugger O'Toole were ranked in the top ten in the list of British middleweights.

A few years later Brendan had another promising black fighter, a heavyweight named Clifton Mitchell. This time Brendan changed Clifton Mitchell into Paddy Reilly and taught him to sing in the ring, 'I'm Big Paddy Reilly from Ballyjamesduff'. Not surprisingly, Mitchell found it ridiculous, even demeaning, and soon reverted to his own name.

The Prince, however, was Naseem's invention. The name grew out of his early sparring sessions with John Ingle. These were in part serious training, in part the fantasy games of youth. John would assume the role, and mimic the style, of one of the legends of the modern ring, while Naseem would be himself, but a glorified version, the Prince or the Arabian Knight: 'In the red corner, fighting out of Brockton, Massachusetts, Marvelous Marvin Hagler; and in the blue corner, fighting out of Sheffield, England, and the Yemen, the Arabian Knight: Prince Naseem Hamed!' The young Naseem was always on about sultans and sheikhs. He claimed that the Queen of Sheba lived in the land that became the Yemen, and took a particular liking to a song on an old gramophone record of Brendan's, 'The Maharajah of Mogador'. Prince Naseem, the Arabian Knight, had all the right associations, Western and Arab, regal and mysterious. The name also allowed for progression to kingship. Before long, it became clear that Prince sufficed and shortly after he turned professional, 'the Arabian Knight', hardly the most original pun, was dropped.

Under the rules of the British Boxing Board of Control, Naseem was eligible to turn professional on 12 February 1992, his eighteenth birthday. He formally did so three weeks later, at a signing ceremony in the House of Commons attended by, among others, an MP named Tony Blair. The venue, arranged by Richard Caborn, Labour MP for Sheffield Central, was another publicity stroke by Brendan. Naseem signed three documents after a reception held by the all-party parliamentary boxing group of MPs. One was a standard three-year Board of Control boxer–manager contract between Brendan and Naseem, under which Brendan was entitled to 25 per cent of Naseem's earnings in the ring; one was a sponsorship contract with Joe Bloggs clothes; the third was a promotional contract with the snooker and boxing impresario, Barry Hearn, stipulating that Naseem would fight exclusively for Hearn, who guaranteed him £1,000 per fight for the first year.

For Naseem, taking on Ricky Beard was no different from taking on the likes of Michael Brodie. And there was no change in Naseem's attitude, despite his sheepishness while Brendan harangued the housewives of Mansfield: Naseem knew he was going to win. Beard had a moderate record but a reputation as a durable fighter who was a big hitter for a flyweight. Naseem entered the ring by vaulting the ropes, wearing an Arab shawl and leopardskin trunks. In the first round he boxed brilliantly but frenetically, sending Beard briefly to the canvas with a left-right combination.

It was the first time Brendan had been in Naseem's corner during a fight, because after he was banned by the ABA, Brendan could not take part in amateur contests in any capacity. He told Naseem to calm down and pick his punches. In the second round, Naseem stalked, Beard covered up. Then Beard made a mistake which – like several of Naseem's subsequent opponents – he soon regretted. He appeared to ridicule Naseem, laughing at him behind his guard. Such laughter is often an attempt to pretend not to have been hurt, a kind of nervous reaction *in extremis*, but Naseem took offence. One punch, a right-handed uppercut to Beard's body, a sickening blow to receive, ended the fight. Naseem concluded with four somersaults and a dance.

Alma Ingle was upstairs at home, ironing. It was ten months after Naseem's first professional contest and his record now read six fights, six wins. All had been easy. Alma could hear Naseem and Ryan Rhodes coming in the side door. A couple of minutes later, she heard Naseem shout in triumph:

'Yes! Eight stone, five pounds! I've had burgers, chips, the lot, and still made it. Yes!'

That was on a Friday evening, after training. Naseem was due to fight Alan Ley, a Welshman who was unbeaten after four fights, at Wembley the following Wednesday, in a match made at eight stone six pounds, the bantamweight limit. The plan was to arrive in London on the Tuesday, with plenty of time to sleep, and get to the weigh-in on the day of the fight.

On the Monday evening, also after training, Naseem again stepped on to the electronic scales in Brendan's living room. This time, Brendan was with him. Eight stone, ten pounds. Four pounds overweight. The day had come, as Brendan had long predicted. No matter how often he had banged on about weight, about the scales being a boxer's most important piece of equipment, he knew, as he often said, that 'Naseem could eat for England'.

Brendan stepped on the scales himself. 'Twelve stone dead,' he announced. 'Listen, we're going down London tomorrow. You've got to lose four pounds and I'm going to lose four pounds as well. Both of us. Have you got me? Go home and have your supper tonight, but don't eat too much. Tomorrow we're going to fast.'

Before Naseem and Brendan set off in Brendan's van the next morning, they weighed themselves again. No difference: Brendan twelve stone, Naseem eight stone ten. They put the scales in the back of the van and stopping only for petrol, no food and no drink, headed for London and the famous boxing pub on the Old Kent Road, the Thomas à Becket.

Brendan and Naseem had a room each there, Brendan on the first floor, the same floor as the gym, Naseem on the floor above. It was February, and freezing. Brendan plugged in the scales and weighed himself. Eleven stone, twelve pounds. He'd lost two pounds on the drive down from Sheffield. Naseem was eight stone, nine. He'd lost a pound.

They had agreed they wouldn't eat or drink, not even water, making a competition out of who could lose the most weight. Brendan lit the gas fire in Naseem's room. There was a sunbed in the corner and he switched that on as well. The more warmth the better. Brendan's room was bitter cold. He went to bed in his clothes but couldn't sleep. He was freezing and he could hear music downstairs in the pub, people leaving at closing time and shouting in the street. At seven the next morning, a gang of labourers arrived outside to lay pipes. They started jack-hammering holes in the pavement.

Brendan lay with his eyes open until eight, then went down to Naseem's room and stood on the scales. Eleven stone eleven. He'd lost another pound overnight. Naseem, bleary and grumpy, got on the scales. He'd lost another pound, too, so he was now two pounds over the limit, with the weigh-in at lunchtime. Brendan went for a pee and then weighed himself again. Eleven stone ten. Another pound gone. Naseem went for a pee. He lost another half a pound. They both went back to bed, wrapped up.

At 9.30, Brendan went back down to Naseem's room. Back on the scales. Another pound gone. He went for another pee. Half a pound. Brendan was winning.

'How can you keep going to the toilet?' said Naseem. 'You must have drunk something.'

'No, as God is my judge,' said Brendan. 'Anyway, if I was drinking, you'd see it on the scales.'

Naseem's turn. Eight stone seven, one pound over. They dressed and went out for a walk, starving and thirsty, but they weren't going to give in now. The weigh-in was at one o'clock and Brendan and Naseem made sure they got there early so they could check Naseem's weight on the official scales. He was a few ounces over, so they went for another walk, striding out. When they got back, Naseem was eight stone five and a half pounds. He'd made it.

Brendan knew it wasn't clever to let on you'd had trouble making the weight. When you saw a boxer step off the scales and down a jug of water or orange juice, you knew his stamina would be suspect. So Brendan took Naseem to one side after the weigh-in and gave him a bottle of a hydrolite sports drink, which was supposed to replace salts as well as liquid.

'Drink it steady,' Brendan said.

Naseem downed it in one and demanded food. They found an Italian restaurant nearby and Naseem ordered spaghetti bolognaise. But with his shrunken stomach, he couldn't eat more than half of it. He ordered a slice of chocolate gâteau but could manage only a couple of spoonfuls.

'I'm going to knock this guy out,' said Naseem. 'He's going to cop for what I've been through. It's not going to go two rounds tonight.'

It didn't. Naseem fought Alan Ley at the Grand Hall, Wembley, on 24 February 1993, seven years to the night after his first contest as a twelve-year-old amateur. Ley was knocked down twice in the first round and twice in the second, after which he remained kneeling, preferring to be counted out rather than stand up and take a further hammering.

The lead-up to the Ley fight suggested that Brendan and Naseem's relationship had changed little. They were in it together, like father and son, teacher and pupil, Svengali and Trilby. But three weeks later Naseem showed he was going his own way and that if Brendan was indeed the father figure, Naseem, like most teenagers, was ready to reject him, to assert himself.

Naseem and Brendan had ended the promotional arrangement with Barry Hearn largely because Brendan feared that Hearn wanted to manage as well as promote Naseem, that he would 'steal' his fighter. So they entered into a similar deal with another promoter, Mickey Duff, this time at terms of £3,000 a fight.

Duff was a member of a syndicate of promoters who had dominated British boxing since the 1970s. As well as furthering Naseem's career, he was giving regular work to Brendan's other boxers, which was how, one evening in March 1993, Brendan came to be sitting with four of his boxers in a dressing room at the Civic Hall in Wolverhampton, at a show promoted by Duff.

Naseem, for once, had stayed in Sheffield. As Brendan and the four boxers got ready, Terry Lawless, one of Duff's partners, came in with the running order. Lee Fox was to go on first, then Clifton Mitchell, followed by Chris Saunders and Neville Brown. That suited Brendan fine, because he reckoned Fox might not win but ought to go the distance and Mitchell had a good chance of knocking out his opponent, which would give Brendan more time to prepare Saunders, who was probably in for a tough fight.

A little later, Duff himself appeared in the dressing room and said that Chris Saunders was to go on second. Brendan said no, Chris

Saunders was on third, it had all been agreed with Terry Lawless. Duff became agitated and began to shout at Brendan. It wasn't his show. He should know better than to make problems. Duff was a past master at hurling abuse, and this was Duff at his highest pitch.

While the tirade continued, Brendan was sitting down, taping Chris Saunders's hands. Saunders was sitting with his back to Duff.

'In any case,' Brendan said when Duff paused for a second, 'Chris Saunders isn't here yet.'

'Why isn't he here?' demanded Duff.

'He's brought a coachload down from Barnsley and he's travelling with them. He should be here soon.'

Duff calmed down and the running order remained unaltered.

The next morning, back in Sheffield, Naseem was waiting for Brendan in the gym. He'd heard all about the episode in Wolverhampton.

'Who got a rollicking last night, then?' Naseem sneered. 'Mickey Bluff tore lumps off you and you stood for it. I'd let no man talk to me like that.'

As Naseem taunted Brendan, sniggering broke out among the others in the gym.

'Wait a second,' said Brendan. 'Mickey was the one with the problem. I got what I wanted. I wasn't going to walk out when I had four boxers on the bill who needed work.'

Naseem shook his head as if to say, that won't wash. He had always been cheeky, and Brendan had never minded being teased: it was a sign of equality. But this was something different. There was a sense of challenge about it. Brendan was hurt by the cruelty, but also embarrassed, because Naseem was right. It was true. He had let Mickey Duff bully him.

But there was another assertion underlying Naseem's taunting of Brendan in his own gym and in front of others. Brendan might be clever, even cunning, and he might be the more experienced, but perhaps Naseem was the one with the stronger personality. Naseem was becoming good at hurting people, physically and mentally. He needed to be, because cruelty is essential in the ring. But now he was finding it gave him power outside the ring as well, and demonstrating that those he was prepared to hurt included Brendan. For both of them, it was a turning point.

# CHAPTER TWELVE

## Brendan, I've Gone and Done It

Brendan was worried. Naseem had done everything asked of him, but now he was going into the unknown. At twenty, he was too young under Board of Control rules to fight for the British title. Instead, after eleven contests as a professional, and never having fought beyond six rounds, he was challenging for the European title, over twelve rounds, and against a proven champion who was one of the toughest bantamweights in the world, Vincenzo Belcastro of Italy.

Frank Warren was worried. He had taken over as Naseem's promoter when the contract with Mickey Duff expired and Naseem had already fought twice on his promotions, winning spectacularly each time. ITV, the terrestrial television network which screened Warren's shows, was delighted with the ratings. Naseem appeared to be the obvious successor to British boxing's fading stars, Frank Bruno, Chris Eubank and Nigel Benn. But even though Warren was not usually the kind of promoter who was over-protective of his best box-office performers, preferring to discover early on whether they could mix it with the best men, he knew he was taking a risk. Belcastro was tough, and just about everyone in boxing reckoned it was a risk Warren was crazy to take. Warren, though, had a hunch that Naseem had the beating of Belcastro. It was a hunch that had to be right.

John Ingle was worried. He remembered Belcastro's last fight, a couple of months before. They were in Brendan's front room – John, Naseem, Brendan and Alma – watching on television as Belcastro defended his title in Glasgow against Drew Docherty, the British champion, who had home-town advantage. Docherty was the man Naseem was expected to meet soon, but Belcastro was the one who impressed. He never took a backward step, hammering Docherty for twelve rounds and making a mess of Docherty's face.

When the fight was over, John and Naseem slipped out of the house to go for a run. As they set off down Newman Road, John said to Naseem: 'If you ever fight that Belcastro, you've got to be fit, superfit. He's done twelve rounds there and he's never stopped throwing punches.'

Naseem's family was worried. They had always supported and encouraged Naseem, and allowed his personality to grow. His mother, Caira, believed him to be a special child. But Naseem's parents had never been enthusiastic about his boxing. Caira, naturally, feared that Naseem might be hurt. When Naseem was about to turn professional, Sal, his father, told the local paper: 'I wish he would give it up. I don't like him boxing, but what can I do? It's his life and it's what he wants to do.' Naseem's brothers knew what was being said around Sheffield, that Naseem had been over-matched against Belcastro, that Brendan and Frank Warren had taken leave of their senses, that they could be destroying a great prospect, that Naseem should fight for the British title first, get used to going eight, ten, twelve rounds before sharing a ring with a man as tough as the European champion. When Naseem's brothers went to Brendan's gym, they found that even the regulars were concerned that this fight might have come too soon.

Naseem was not worried. He told them all, his family, John, Brendan, Frank Warren, anyone who wanted to know: 'I'm going to bash him up.'

Frank Warren had been watching Naseem's progress for some time before he was able to sign him up. Warren remembered seeing Naseem a couple of times as an amateur, and saw his early professional fights on television. For Warren, 'the kid had something – skill, reflexes, a great eye. He was a cheeky little sod but you could see it was all there'. But that was during the period when Warren's life had been torn to pieces, almost ended. On 30 November 1989 he had been shot outside the Broadway Theatre in Barking. Four bullets entered his chest. After emergency surgery, he survived despite losing half a lung. His business, which included the ownership and management of the London Arena stadium in east London, collapsed, and he found

63

himself several million pounds in debt. Warren, who had often surprised and taken advantage of those who had underestimated him, even written him off, climbed off the floor. He built up his boxing business again, promoting shows all over Britain, signing up several of the leading fighters and continuing to supply fights for ITV. By Christmas 1993, Warren had established himself as the number one promoter in Britain.

Warren, who kept an eye on up-and-coming talent, was surprised that Naseem was not more forcefully and frequently projected. Perhaps Mickey Duff was losing his touch. In any case, when Warren heard that Duff's contract with Naseem had expired, he moved. Warren invited Brendan and Naseem to his country home in the Hertfordshire green belt.

The three of them hit it off from the start. Brendan and Naseem were immediately impressed by being invited to Warren's home rather than his office. It was a calculated move but not a cynical one. Warren liked to meet fighters in informal surroundings; he introduced Brendan and Naseem to his wife and children and showed them around the house and grounds.

Warren knew exactly how to make his pitch. He told Brendan he was aware that Hearn and Duff had wanted to get involved in managing as well as promoting Naseem, but that he did not: 'I'll promote him, you manage him, and let him do the hard bit in the ring. I won't steal him off you.'

Warren was also impressed by Naseem's confidence. From their first conversation, Naseem made it clear he was going to win a world title. Naseem had never seen a house like Warren's. It was a mansion and play-palace with indoor swimming pool, full-size snooker table and a Wrangler jeep outside on the gravel. 'The jeep's yours when you win the world title,' said Warren.

When Naseem and Brendan left Warren's house and headed back up the motorway to Sheffield, they were both excited. The deal was a good one. Naseem was guaranteed twice the amount per fight he had earned from Duff. At a stroke, the money had become substantial enough to become an issue.

'There's something on my mind,' said Naseem after a period of silence. 'I don't want you to take 25 per cent from my sponsorships and endorsements.'

'Don't move the goalposts,' said Brendan. 'I'm your manager and I'm entitled to 25 per cent of what you earn in the ring and from sponsorships. Who was it who got your Joe Bloggs deal?'

But Naseem insisted. He didn't want Brendan to share in endorsements or sponsorships. He could have 25 per cent of ring earnings but that was all. Brendan didn't like it, but he agreed.

Naseem's purse for challenging Vincenzo Belcastro for the European title was £12,500. He knew as well as Brendan and Frank Warren that this was a make-or-break fight. There was also a nagging concern in his mind: not whether he would win, but whether he might struggle to go twelve rounds. He had seen enough in the gym and at fights over the years to know that twelve rounds of sparring was quite different from twelve rounds of real combat.

Never before or since have Naseem and Brendan worked so closely together for a shared objective – getting Naseem ready to fight twelve rounds flat out, to beat Belcastro. For three weeks, they went into training camp. Brendan arranged for the use of two bedrooms at a complex belonging to Rotherham United Football Club. Every day, Brendan and Naseem followed the same routine: up at 8.30, or as near to 8.30 as Naseem could manage; breakfast of cornflakes; drive to the gym in Newman Road to train from 9.45 until noon; on to the Post House hotel for a sauna and jacuzzi; back to Newman Road to drop off Naseem at the shop, where he handed his mother his dirty gear to be washed, then disappeared for an afternoon nap; back to the gym at 5 to train until 6.30; return to the training ground for supper; run round the pitches together for twenty minutes or so; shower and in bed by 10.30.

After three weeks, they were sick of the sight of each other. Brendan's biggest problem was dragging Naseem out of bed. There was nothing new in that. Naseem loved his sleep. When Naseem first turned professional, Brendan thought it would be a good idea to go running with Naseem at six or seven in the morning. That's what he had done himself as a pro, and that's what most pros did, if they were serious. But Brendan eventually tired of hanging around outside, trying to find pieces of gravel that were big enough to chuck as high as Naseem's bedroom window in the attic, but not so big that they might break the glass.

Naseem was never fitter than against Belcastro. He made the bantamweight limit for the first time since starving himself for the fight against Alan Ley. In sparring he was untouchable, handling heavier men – even Johnny Nelson, who was more than four stone heavier – with ease.

On 11 May 1994 Naseem fought Belcastro at the Ponds Forge Centre in Sheffield. It was Naseem's first fight in his home town as a professional. Brendan led Naseem to the ring, knowing that he had never had in his charge a more skilful or better boxer, or one more powerful for his weight. For Brendan, Naseem was close to being the perfect fighter.

Statistically and physically, Naseem and Belcastro provided a remarkable contrast. Belcastro was thirty-three. He had taken part in fourteen title fights from national to world level over the full twelve-round distance. He was unbeaten in three years and was ranked sixth in the world by the World Boxing Council. In the ring, he looked a hard nugget, a small, swarthy, muscular man with his head shaved save for a strip of close-cropped hair running from his forehead to the back of his neck. In the street he would be a man to watch and keep away from, and it was no surprise he had a reputation for fighting tough and dirty.

Naseem had never fought for a professional title, had never fought over twelve rounds and was unconsidered at world level. He was twenty, but looked younger, his complexion smooth, his hair cut with an old-fashioned parting. It was a man against a boy.

As the fight commenced, Jim Watt, the ITV commentator and former world lightweight champion, went straight to the heart of the matter. Watt had often criticised Naseem's unorthodox style and hinted that at a higher level Naseem might be exposed. 'Now we will find out how good Hamed is,' Watt told the viewers as Hamed circled around Belcastro. There wasn't long to wait. After twenty-five seconds of round one, Naseem jumped in on Belcastro, hit him with a straight-left, straight-right combination, and Belcastro tumbled to the canvas for the first time in his career.

Hit and avoid getting hit was Brendan's first principle of pugilism, and it was never better demonstrated. Naseem, apparently off balance, incorrect, awkward, yet the opposite of all three, rendered Belcastro a stumbling invalid. Belcastro recovered his senses quickly from the first knockdown (although his attempt to appear unruffled fooled no one), only to suffer a further eleven rounds of perplexity and pain. In the fifth, a heavy left from Naseem caused Belcastro to stumble. In the eighth, a terrible succession of body-punches forced the Italian to wince and drop his arms for protection. In the eleventh, Belcastro fell victim to Naseem's party trick: Naseem looked down intently at Belcastro's boots as if he had spotted something of value, and without shifting his gaze fired a right-hand punch, straight and angled skywards, to Belcastro's chin. Again, Belcastro fell to the canvas and again he hauled himself to his feet to take some more.

True to his reputation, Belcastro attempted a mixture of fair and foul. He was completely outboxed, and since he found it all but impossible to strike Naseem with the gloved fist in the approved target area, it was hard for him to resist catching Naseem low a few times and using his head as a weapon in the clinches. It was a head-butt that opened up a crimson gash below Naseem's left eye and another that produced a slit above his right.

Such was Naseem's mastery that there was more than a suspicion that he could have finished off Belcastro inside the distance. But Naseem was intent on proving he could go twelve rounds and chose to play with his prey.

When he returned to his corner at the end of the eleventh round, with energy left to spare, and Belcastro a beaten wreck, Naseem was ecstatic.

'What d'you reckon?' Naseem said to Brendan as he towelled him down. He wasn't asking how he was doing, he was saying, well what do you reckon to that, am I not brilliant?

'Naz, you've done it,' said Brendan. 'He's hit you in the balls, he's butted you, he's tried all sorts, but you've done it. One round left: go out, stay out of trouble, and enjoy yourself.'

For the first couple of minutes of the final round, Naseem boxed at distance, staying out of range and proving that his legs remained strong and elastic. Only a knockout could deny him, and Belcastro was incapable of summoning such a blow.

In the last minute, Naseem began to ridicule Belcastro. He threw his hands high in the air, then placed them on his gyrating hips. He offered his chin for a free shot, stuck out his tongue, shuffled his legs Ali-style, and pretended to talk to Brendan in the corner, and a television cameraman at ringside. At first, Belcastro plodded after his tormentor. That was futile, so he tried to imitate the mickey-taker, mimicking Naseem's antics. What Belcastro couldn't do, as Naseem demonstrated, was hit Naseem, even when Naseem stood in front of him with no defence and his tongue stuck out.

At the final bell, Naseem went back to the corner. 'Brendan, I've gone and done it,' he said. And he had. He was way ahead on the scorecards of all three judges, only one of whom thought he had lost a single round.

The chief effect of Naseem's behaviour in the last of the thirty-six minutes of the engagement was to invite the disapproval, almost loathing, of most sports writers and commentators. For making a fool of Belcastro, Naseem was charged with demeaning the noble art. Typical was Hugh McIlvanney, probably the most celebrated British boxing writer, who wrote in the *Sunday Times* that Naseem had 'polluted' the final round by treating Belcastro 'as if he were no better than something you wipe off your shoe'.

Naseem undoubtedly went over the top in his exuberance. He was only twenty, after all. But the views of his critics seemed equally extreme, even ludicrous, since they were based on a knights-of-the-round-table view of boxing as combat between heroic figures sharing mutual respect. Such a position required the elevation of Belcastro to the status of the fallen but admirable champion, the upholder of boxing's virtues, which was ridiculous, given his tactics.

In some cases, the attacks on Naseem served to excuse those who made them from admitting just how astonishing his performance had been. For those who had never taken Brendan's extravagant claims for Naseem seriously, it was hard to admit they had seen a man who might not merely join the short list of post-war British fighters who had been truly world class – Randolph Turpin, Howard Winstone, Ken Buchanan, John Conteh, Barry McGuigan – but could outshine them all.

For the moment, they were as much in the dark as Belcastro, who, speaking little English, left his manager to give his verdict: 'Vincenzo does not understand what this Hamed was doing. He does not know if Hamed understood what he was doing. He thinks Hamed should learn to box normally.'

The public had a different view. The Belcastro fight marked the beginning of Naseem as a cult figure, especially among the young and hip, many of whom knew nothing of boxing. ITV executives realised they were on to a winner, and would be astonished by the audience figures they were to achieve with Naseem's next five fights. Frank Warren had been vindicated in his belief that Naseem had the beating of Belcastro. As far as he was concerned, the last round had been 'Naseem just showing how good he was'.

Brendan would always remember the fight that made Naseem as one of the highlights of his life in boxing, a performance close to perfection, by the most skilful boxer he had known, trained to a point where power, speed and stamina were harmonious.

It was a turning point, too, for Naseem's family, who, since the fight was in Sheffield, had attended in force. They were swiftly coming to the heady realisation that what Brendan had been telling them for some time – that Naseem would make millions – might well be true.

For Naseem himself there was exhilaration and particular pleasure that he had lasted twelve rounds easily. There was also a naive bewilderment in the face of criticism. He failed to see that it wasn't smart to give ammunition to the enemy.

'I was twenty years of age and on paper I didn't have a chance,' Naseem said a few days later. 'He had just beaten the British champion easy. I bamboozled him, outboxed him, outpowered him. I was so happy when that twelfth round came, I went out to have a good time.'

He had a bonus, too. He may only have won a European rather than a world title, but Frank Warren gave him the jeep.

# CHAPTER THIRTEEN
## Brendan's Last Stand

Naseem was in the dressing room, getting ready. There were fifteen minutes to go before he was due to make his entrance in his first defence of the European bantamweight title, which, like the Belcastro fight, was held in Sheffield.

In the auditorium, a six-round preliminary contest was in progress. One of Brendan's boxers was involved and Brendan and John Ingle were in his corner. Frank Warren, the promoter of the show, wondered how Naseem, the star attraction, was getting on and made his way from the auditorium at the Hillsborough Leisure Centre to the aerobics studio at the back which was being used as one of the dressing rooms.

Warren had often watched fighters as they made their last preparations. Some were hyperactive, working themselves into a frenzy of aggression. Others were quiet, grave, seeking resolution. A few were plain frightened. But Warren had never seen anything like this: Naseem was alone, dancing to music. And it wasn't just limbering up, keeping the muscles loose. It was a one-man rave.

Naseem was always relaxed before a contest, a most unusual and happy state of mind that served him well because tension is the fighter's enemy, draining confidence and energy, cramping movement. If anyone was tense, it was Warren, probably out of habit.

'Don't worry, Frank. This is what I'm going to do: I'm going to walk out and first off I'm going to feint with the left and lead with the right uppercut.' Naseem demonstrated the shot. 'That'll do his head in. Then I'll box through the first round, switching, looking good. Second round, same, and he'll go in the third. And watch when he goes down – that's when I'll do the somersault.'

And that, to Warren's astonishment, was precisely how Naseem dealt with Antonio Picardi, a durable opponent rated the number one challenger by the European Boxing Union. The right uppercut lead narrowly missed its target, but it succeeded in putting Picardi into a fixed state of trepidation. Picardi made four visits to the canvas before the referee stopped the fight halfway through the third round. Naseem, who had climbed into the ring through the ropes in the regulation manner, and without his gold gown – a token response to the criticisms that followed the Belcastro fight – was into his somersault before the referee had finished waving his arms.

For his next fight, Naseem went up a weight, to super-bantamweight (the eight stone, ten pounds division), and up a class, taking on Freddy Cruz of the Dominican Republic, who was reputed to be one of the toughest fighters in the world among the lighter weights. In fifty-six contests, Cruz had never been stopped. It was said he had never even been floored, and his only two losses in the previous six years had been against world champions, Wilfredo Vazquez and Steve Robinson.

Cruz was the kind of opponent who might upset Naseem. Defeating him was no major challenge – he held no terrors and no title – but he was experienced and might be good enough to take advantage if Naseem was complacent. Certainly, Naseem's training was poor in comparision with the work he did before facing Belcastro. Naseem had unilaterally decided to give up regular running, often returning to the gym late at night in compensation, before going to bed in the early hours and rising at ten in the morning. Naseem's explanation was that he was a night person, and it was true that the training he did, especially his sparring, was still of the best quality, often sensational. But Naseem had won a little battle with Brendan. He was training when it suited him, not when he was told.

But whatever chance Cruz might have had of springing a surprise vanished when he inadvertently raised the devil in Naseem. At the final pre-fight press conference, an occasion when a few insults and boasts are traditionally exchanged for publicity purposes, Cruz touched Naseem gently on the cheek, and said, through his manager, who interpreted: 'I thought I was coming to fight a man. I am not sure I can fight with a child. I don't want to end up in jail.'

It seared a nerve. When Naseem was called Paki or nigger he felt contempt for the ignorance betrayed. Such insults didn't disturb him. But when he was called a child or a boy he took violent and personal offence. Belittling Naseem produced such anger that it suggested a psychological reaction deeper than wounded pride. It summoned in Naseem a ruthless determination and an inclination towards cruelty. Cruz was not the last opponent to make the mistake; nor the last to suffer for it.

Naseem usually preferred to pose in the first round and get down to business in the second. For Cruz, he reserved a different approach. Cruz was hurt very early and continually, so that when he went back to his corner at the end of the first round, he held out his hand as if to acknowledge that Naseem had made his point. If the gesture was designed to placate Naseem, it had no effect, for there would be no respite. Naseem was relentless. And it wasn't that he was slugging. He was boxing at his best.

As Cruz sat on his stool, his manager asked him: 'Why aren't you throwing any punches?'

'I don't know where he is,' Cruz said. 'First I see him on the right. Then he's behind me on the left. What happened?'

Cruz's torture continued until the sixth round, when he was finally finished off. Naseem feinted with the left, and brought up the right uppercut, catching Cruz cleanly to the face. Cruz remained upright but some way short of full consciousness. After a further attack and another uppercut, the referee intervened. For the first time in fifty-seven fights, Cruz had been beaten inside the distance. 'He called me a child,' said Naseem when he summed up. 'He had to take his punishment.'

When ITV replayed the telling punch in slow motion, Jim Watt, previously a sceptic, seemed lost in wonder. 'Hamed seems to have the ability to change the direction of a punch after he starts to throw it,' Watt said. 'That looked as though it came out as a jab and he just

73

switched it into an uppercut, bang on the chin. I've never seen that before.'

Brendan smiled when he replayed the fight on video and heard Watt's remark. He had seen the punch before, many times, thrown with the left as well as the right. It was the one that used to knock the wind out of troublesome men in Dublin pubs just after the war, the one that landed on the third button of the waistcoat.

Coming up to Christmas 1994, Naseem had fought fifteen, won fifteen. Ryan Rhodes, his mate, who was two and a half years younger, was soon to turn professional. They were Brendan's golden boys. Both had been taught by Brendan from childhood; both went to the gym every day without fail from the start; both won several schoolboy and junior amateur titles.

A few years before, when Naseem was sixteen and Ryan thirteen, they had a hard sparring session and Ryan was hurt. He started crying. Brendan took Ryan to one side and said, 'Listen, one day you'll be bigger than him and you'll hold your own, he won't be able to dominate you.'

That day had not quite come, but it was not far off. Even then, just before Ryan's professional début, it wasn't a good idea to allow Ryan and Naseem to spar together, because they might be best friends but neither would give an inch. Each of them would rather die than be licked, and if they really went at it, one of them might never be the same again as a fighter. Which one, was anybody's guess.

'We want more sparring,' Naseem demanded after a hard session when he and Ryan had been taking on all-comers.

'That's your lot. Finish,' said Brendan, from his steps by the ring. Even with the gym's house rule of body-sparring only, no shots to the head, Brendan had to be careful about who sparred with whom, and how much sparring each boxer should do. Short bursts of high quality were always of more value than prolonged sessions, and most fighters wanted to do too much.

'More sparring,' Ryan chimed in.

'You've been through everybody. Finish,' said Brendan.

'You get in, then,' said Naseem.

'Me? You wouldn't have lasted when I was fighting,' said Brendan. 'I'd have walked through the pair of you.'

'No way,' said Naseem, who then came out with a taunt that he knew never failed to needle Brendan. 'You were only a six-round fighter. You never even won an area title.'

'If I had been looked after as well as you two have been looked after, I'd never have lost,' said Brendan.

A famous American trainer and cuts man, Jackie McCoy, once noted of former boxers that 'no matter how old they are, they still think they can fight'. In his sensible moments, Brendan knew the truth of that, but now his blood was up. He was fed up with the moaning, fed up that Naseem kept saying he couldn't fight.

Brendan, aged fifty-four, took off his shirt, hauled himself into the ring and gloved up. First he sparred a round with Ryan, aged eighteen, followed by a round with Naseem, aged twenty, and then back to Ryan. When Ryan was sparring against Brendan, Naseem egged him on. When Naseem was in with Brendan, Ryan did the same. Brendan, without a break, did six rounds with each, twelve in all, and he was bashed up. It was body-sparring only, but Brendan couldn't cover everything. If he protected his stomach by leaning over like an old woman with a bundle, they whacked him round the sides. And when he tried to hit back, he missed, or if he landed, they laughed. Brendan wouldn't stop for pride, and all the while he was thinking, you bastards, I wish I was younger.

Towards the end of it, John Ingle came into the gym. He could hardly believe what he saw. John had sparred with Naseem for years, but had given up after a painful session over two years before. John was two stones heavier than Naseem, but Naseem did a job on him, working him over, busting his lip, hurting him to the body until John said: 'That's it. That's me done with you.'

Now here was Brendan, his father, taking on not just Naseem but Ryan as well, and they were pulling him around like two dogs attacking an old and injured bear.

Finally, Brendan called a halt. 'I've just done over half an hour, twelve rounds, with the two of you and I'm still standing. Let's see what you can do when you're fifty-four.'

Brendan held out a glove for John to unlace. He took off the gloves, clambered out of the ring and walked through the gym to the door. When he shut the door behind him, he bent double and staggered across the road to his house. There was no one in. Brendan crawled upstairs, knelt and ran a bath, and shook a whole packet of Epsom salts into the water. He climbed in and lay soaking.

After a while, Alma came home. She called up the stairs: 'Are you in?'

'I'm in the bath.'

It was late afternoon, hardly bath-time, so Alma went upstairs and saw Brendan, shamefaced, with lumps and bruises all over his body.

'You've been sparring, haven't you?'

'I have.'

'You're mad.'

## Ryan Rhodes's Story

*I started in the gym when I was six. I was fighting on the streets and getting in trouble. My mum took me down to the market in Sheffield city centre one day. Herol Graham had a jewellery shop there and he said to bring me down to the gym. I started with Brendan's Saturday-morning classes and I loved boxing straight away. I took to it. I met Naz a few weeks later. He had started about a year earlier and was ahead of me. We were friends from the beginning and we've always wanted each other to do well. We've had some battles, but these days we don't spar full out because it wouldn't do either of us any good. So it's not really a competition between us. It's practice. We try different moves but not with full power.*

*Brendan taught me the rights and wrongs, life and social skills. He's been like a father to me, to all of us. I know that if I wasn't boxing, I'd be knocking around with the kids I went to school with, and a lot of them are in prison. I wasn't at all brainy at school and I made boxing the main object of my life. My friends thought I was an idiot. Lads would say, let's go and play football or* mess about, but I'd say, no, I'm going training. I never missed it. I did go out with girls, but the boxing always came first. These days, some of my old friends even ask for my autograph. It's weird. I won four national amateur titles, two schoolboy national titles, a junior national title and a national boys' clubs title. I had sixty-seven amateur fights and lost eleven and most of those losses were because the officials.didn't like Brendan.

I turned pro at eighteen. What the commentators don't realise when we get in with people who are twenty-eight or twenty-nine is that Naz and me have had as much experience as them because we've been in the gym since we were six or seven, and we've been everywhere, all over England, Wales and Scotland, and abroad with Brendan, learning the game. When I was fourteen, I went over to Spain with Brendan and Naz and everyone when Herol Graham fought Julian Jackson. I was gutted when he lost. But when Herol got to the top, he must have thought he didn't need Brendan. From when they split up, Herol was never right. It was as if something was missing, and that something was Brendan.

I took my first pro fight too lightly. It was in Wales against a big puncher, Lee Crocker. In the dressing room, I was more worried about how my hair looked than the fight. I looked in the mirror and it was standing up. Brendan spat on his hand and smarmed it down. Then on the way to the ring, there was no music. I complained to Brendan: how can I dance when there's no music? Where's my music? I wasn't focused on the fight at all, and when the bell went Crocker chinned me. I was up at the count of four and he chinned me again, for another four count.

At the end of the round, Brendan gave me a rollicking: You're worrying about your hair and your music. You're not playing marbles here. Now go out and get rid of him. Frank Warren came round to the corner as well and he gave me a rollicking. I went out for the second round with my hands up and I put him away.

Since then I've learned to relax but switch on when the bell goes. That's my signal. The bell means it's time for business. I won a Lonsdale belt in record time. You have to win a British title and successfully defend it twice to win the belt. The big one for me was winning the title when I beat Silky Jones. He used to train in our gym and he knows most of our moves, so it was a hard fight. In fact, when I was about thirteen, Silky put me down in sparring. We *were messing about and I had a go at him and he hit me on the chin and put me down. I got up to have a go back but Brendan called time. But what Silky didn't know was that we have advanced our training since he left. When Silky was in the gym, we used to have this move where we'd duck on to our haunches and roll our heads as we stood back up, with our eyes looking down. But now we roll back up with our eyes looking up, ready to punch, or to get out of the way. It takes a bit of practice. I got my own back on Silky. It was very even until the eighth round. Then he rolled like we used to, with his eyes down, and I caught him, hit him with a straight left and I knew he was hurt straight away.*

*I'm loving every minute of my boxing. I do get hit but I don't feel the pain. It's hard to explain. You're that psyched up in the ring that you don't think about it. The only times I've been hurt is in the amateurs, being hurt inside when I know I've won and not got the decision. But we've all had it – me, Naz, everyone. I know that Naz and me are not one-offs. There are others who are as good in our gym, and there'll be more to come.*

*The first fight I lost as a pro was for the world title, against Otis Grant, on points. I was twenty-one and I know I'll get better. I want to be a world champion at three weights: light-middle, middle and super-middle. But success won't change me. I just want to be financially secure with my family. I don't want to be stinking rich.*

# CHAPTER FOURTEEN

## It's Like Aladdin

Naseem was standing on the rooftops, high above the souk in Sana'a, the capital city of the Yemen. He leaned over to peer at the throng below. A jostling, fevered crowd was looking upwards, thousands of eyes focused on a single object and all hands pointing skywards, to him, every mouth was chanting 'Naseem! Naseem!'

This was unbelievable. Naseem had visited the country of his parents' birth two years before, and that had been wild enough. He had attracted several thousand spectators when he put on sparring exhibitions. He had also been given a gold Rolex watch worth £10,000 and a ceremonial dagger by the Yemen's military ruler, President General Ali Abdullah Salah. The party on that occasion included Alma Ingle, who found her first visit to a third world country an awful experience. She was shocked to see people living in shacks, in shelters made from oil drums and corrugated iron, and terrified when the army and police beat people back, hitting their legs with sticks.

But now, on his second visit, Naseem was royalty. His recent fights had been broadcast on Yemeni television, and the ten million inhabitants of a desert country twice the size of England, Scotland and Wales, had identified a national, international hero. Whether the President General followed the trend or started it, it suited his purpose. Naseem's portrait was on the country's stamps. It was on government-issue school exercise books. The big club football competition had even been renamed the Naseem Cup.

Naseem and his entourage, which included Frank Warren, Brendan, Naseem's parents, three of his brothers and Johnny Nelson, were given a military escort from the airport. At an audience with the President General, whose residence was more fort than palace, Naseem received the Order of Merit, first class, the Yemen's highest civilian decoration.

When Naseem staged another sparring exhibition, 30,000 came to idolise. At the final of the Naseem Cup, 80,000 spectators paid homage and the players queued for Naseem's autograph before the kick-off.

In the twisting, narrow streets of the souk, on a walkabout with guards brandishing automatic rifles, Naseem was mobbed. An amble became a trot, a stall laden with dates was overturned, and Naseem was forced to seek refuge on the roof. As dusk softened another day of searing heat, the crowd chanted his name in their happiness: 'Naseem! Naseem!'

Naseem turned to Frank Warren. 'They love me,' he said. 'Look, they love me. Hey Frank, it's like Aladdin, ain't it?'

There was still the problem of making it back to the car. Warren solved it by throwing a bundle of notes of local currency into the air while they made a dash for it.

Six weeks later, on 6 May 1995, in his eighteenth professional fight, Naseem defeated Enrique Angeles of Mexico, the referee intervening in the second round, in front of 5,500 wildly cheering fans crammed into the sweltering agricultural hall at the Royal Bath and West Showground, Shepton Mallet.

In the immediate afterglow, Naseem looked straight to a shoulder-mounted television camera and said: 'That was a beautiful workout. Oh baby, I'm feeling so good.'

Frank Warren, also interviewed as Angeles rearranged his senses in the ring above, was sweating almost as much as Naseem. He was equally excited. The words gushed out, for Warren had been carried beyond the calculated semi-formal tone he normally adopted in front of camera. 'He's got so much juice in him and you've not seen any of it yet,' Warren spurted. 'There's so much in reserve. He's the best fighter I've ever seen.' This was not selling, but pure abandon. A fleeting sign of embarrassment crossed Warren's face, suggesting that he realised his enthusiasm had perhaps taken him a fence too far. He paused, seeming to consider whether he should qualify his last statement. He let it stand.

If 1994 was the year of breakthrough, 1995 was the year of

realisation, the year that changed Naseem's life. It was the year he turned twenty-one; the year he became famous, not in one country but in two; it was the year he became very rich; the year he declared he was favoured by God. It was also, he knew, the year he would become world champion.

Of all the changing aspects of Naseem's life, the most dramatic, and fortuitous, concerned money. For beating Angeles – the beautiful workout – he was paid far in excess of the combined purses he had received for his seventeen previous professional appearances. The reason, and the reason that Naseem and Frank Warren were quite so pumped up after another Latin American boxer had predictably been deposited on the canvas, was that the fight was televised not by ITV, as originally scheduled, but by Sky, the satellite station controlled by Rupert Murdoch. The change of broadcaster was no token matter, for both Frank Warren and Naseem could count its significance in millions of pounds.

Warren had left the Yemen a week before Naseem. He flew to the United States at the invitation of Don King, who was holding a party to celebrate Mike Tyson's release from prison after serving a sentence for rape. Warren and King had become promotional partners in September 1994. For twenty years, King had been the most brilliant and controversial personality in boxing. Warren and King shared an odd coincidence: both had been involved in close-range, civilian shootings, though from opposite ends of the gun. Perhaps that was significant. The partnership was to break up in spectacular bitterness, but at the outset it was mutually beneficial and extravagantly cordial.

After the party for Tyson, Warren quickly returned to London. He had been contacted by Sam Chisholm, the chief executive of BSkyB. Chisholm had a proposition to put to Warren, and it wasn't one to discuss on the telephone, or even in Chisholm's office, where Warren's presence would doubtless be noted. Chisholm invited Warren to his London flat.

It wasn't hard for Warren to guess what the proposition might be, and how it might benefit him. Buying up the rights to televised sport in Britain was the main hook by which Sky aimed to persuade viewers to buy a satellite dish and subscribe. In 1992, Sky paid £304 million for the rights to Premier League football. Subsequently, Sky moved into cricket, rugby union and golf. Boxing was the next big prize.

When he arrived at Chisholm's flat, Warren knew he had a strong hand to play, and he had done his homework. Through his connections with King, he could deliver Tyson's eagerly awaited comeback fights. He could also deliver the cream of British talent. Warren could recite off pat the recent viewing figures for his top three attractions, Frank Bruno, Nigel Benn and Naseem. Their fights screened on ITV had been among the top-rated sports programmes on any channel over the previous year. Naseem's most recent fight, against the almost unknown Sergio Liendo in Livingston, a small town near Edinburgh, late on a Saturday night in March, had attracted an astonishing 9.5 million viewers for ITV. Enthusiasm for Naseem had spread well beyond the base of those normally interested in boxing. Naseem, like Tyson, was one of those rare fighters the public would watch regardless of his opponent.

But Chisholm, a New Zealander regarded in the television industry as a legendary deal-maker, needed no persuasion. He was buying, and he came straight to the point.

'We want your boxing.'

'How much will you pay me for it?' asked Warren.

'Not so fast. I don't want to make you an offer just so that you can go back to ITV and use it to get more money from them.'

'No, don't worry. I'm not looking for an auction. Make me an offer, a realistic offer.'

Within half an hour, the most significant deal in the history of boxing on British television was done. The exact terms were kept secret, but for the exclusive rights to televise Warren's promotions over a two-year period, Sky are reckoned to have paid £50 million.

Sky had secured a near-monopoly overnight. Warren was not only back in business in a big way, but looking ahead to the enticing prospect of pay-per-view. The objective of every promoter is to increase ticket revenues. In the old days, only those who bought tickets and sat inside the stadium could watch a big fight live. In the 1960s and

1970s, during the heyday of Muhammad Ali, promoters developed a way to effectively extend the stadium, and the reaches of the ticket office, by beaming live pictures to cinemas around the world. But the ultimate extension of the stadium is pay-per-view television, which was already well established in the United States but had not been launched in Britain. Pay-per-view is the promoter's sweetest dream: millions of patrons sitting at home, watching the fight and buying a ticket for the privilege.

Another effect of the Sky deal, and one of the many consequences of Rupert Murdoch's determination to make a success of his satellite channel, was to instantly make Naseem a millionaire. The progression of his earnings was amazing. When Naseem first turned professional, he was paid £1,000 each for his first three contests. His purses gradually increased until he was paid £6,000 for his tenth fight. When he fought for the European title, against Belcastro, he was paid £12,500. His purses rose sharply again until he was paid over £50,000 for the Liendo fight, his last for ITV. By then, his seventeen purses, over three years of fighting, amounted to less than £250,000. After the first fight for Sky, against Angeles, Naseem's career earnings had more than doubled. Two years later, the figure would be in excess of £5 million.

Even before Naseem's sudden good fortune, divisions with Brendan had arisen. The first rift had come when Naseem signed a promotional contract with Frank Warren and told Brendan he didn't want him to share in sponsorship deals as well as ring earnings, an arrangement Brendan accepted but resented.

Next, it was Naseem's turn to feel aggrieved. After the Belcastro fight, Brendan told Naseem he intended to take advantage of a Board of Control rule that allowed managers to unilaterally extend a contract with a boxer after he won a title. The purpose of the rule was to protect managers from having their boxers poached once they had taken them to the top.

But Naseem was shocked that such a rule should exist and even more shocked that Brendan should choose to exercise it: 'You'll always be my manager. Don't you trust me?'

Brendan said he was going to do it anyway, that it was his only protection, and he wrote off to the Board of Control. The original three-year contract, which had been running for less than two and a half years, was extended for a further two years. Naseem, as well as Brendan, now harboured a resentment.

The advent of more money is always likely to make such disagreements worse and the most serious and lasting division arose after the Sky deal. Once Frank Warren had his own contract in place, he offered Naseem a new long-term promotional deal. It involved Naseem's next ten fights and was worth several million pounds, to be paid in instalments, fight by fight, as long as Naseem kept winning.

Soon after the new contract was agreed, Naseem told Brendan he didn't want to pay him 25 per cent, but a fee for each fight. Brendan worked out that the fee Naseem suggested was just 16 per cent. For Brendan, it was Naseem moving the goalposts again.

For years, Brendan had anticipated that something of the sort would happen. He had a story, a kind of parable he often told and often in public, about how he raised the issue with Naseem when he was twelve years old.

'Me and Naz were travelling back in the car one night after he had boxed. I said to Naz, you and me are going to make a lot of money. Now let's go on a few years and imagine what might happen. You're eighteen, so what are you going to do? And he said, I'm going pro with you, Brendan. Right, I said. It's your first fight. You're on £400 and I get 25 per cent. How much do you get and how much do I get? And he said, I'm on £300 and you're on £100. All right, I said, let's go on. You're twenty and you're boxing for the British title. You're on £4,000. What do you get and what do I get? I get £3,000, he said, and you get £1,000. So I said to him, what d'you reckon to that? And he said, that's a lot of money, £1,000, Brendan. Let's go on another four years, I said. We're in Las Vegas. You're fighting for the world title. You're on £400,000. Now what do you get and what do I get? I get £300,000 and you get £100,000, he said. Then he said, Oh, I don't agree with that, Brendan – £100,000 is a lot of money. So I said to him, I ought to chuck you out of the car, you ungrateful little bastard. By that time, I'd have spent sixteen years on you.'

Sometimes, Brendan would add a significant conclusion to the story: 'A few weeks later, in the gym, Naseem came up to me and said, I've been talking to my dad, Brendan. You can have the £100,000.'

For Brendan, it had all come true. He was going to be ripped off, just as he had predicted. But it wasn't that simple. There was also a strong case against Brendan getting the full manager's entitlement. Naseem had a long-term promotional contract with Frank Warren so there was no need for Brendan to negotiate terms for fights. In reality, Warren managed Naseem's career and Brendan's role had been reduced to that of Naseem's trainer. Trainers received 10 per cent of a boxer's purse at the most, so how could a slice of 25 per cent be justified? And even if Brendan had taught Naseem from an early age, and had been given a promise by Naseem when he was twelve, did that mean Naseem was beholden for life?

But Brendan could counter by arguing that his relationship with Naseem had never been the usual one between a boxer and his manager. He had spent many years developing him. He had taken him all over the country, and abroad, fed him, looked after him like a son. Their dream and their understanding all along was that they would both make their fortunes.

Nevertheless, however strong his objections were, Brendan again accepted Naseem's terms. He didn't have to, because their contract was still in force and he had a right to a straight 25 per cent of Naseem's earnings in the ring. But he agreed.

When they got back to Sheffield after signing the new contract with Frank Warren, Brendan and Naseem sat down with an accountant and worked out how much Brendan would be paid for each fight, and how and when it would be paid. Brendan accepted 16 per cent, but he never became reconciled to it. He felt cheated and betrayed, and that meant trouble ahead.

# CHAPTER FIFTEEN
## A Gift from God

After his first fight for Sky, Naseem did not return immediately to Sheffield, to the gym, or to his attic room above the shop in Newman Road, which was still his home. Instead, he gave himself a four-week treat, staying in a £3,000-a-week suite at the Dorchester Hotel in London, shopping by day, clubbing by night. Finally, in early June 1995, he returned and began training for his next fight, against a Colombian, Juan Polo Perez, a former world champion at super-flyweight.

You could go away from Brendan's gym, the smell of the place and the jangle of movement and music fresh in your brain, and return a month, a year, ten years later, and it would all be the same. On a late Thursday afternoon four weeks before the fight, Naseem was sparring up in the ring under the strip lights. He went twenty rounds with three sparring partners taking their turn – Wayne Windell, who had joined the gym about the same time as Naseem, Kevin Adamson, a middleweight, and Johnny Nelson, cruiserweight. Naseem moved fast, always with intent, choosing when to be in range, and when he was, he stood toe to toe, banging, never yielding an inch to the heavier man. He was punching harder than ever. The string-puppet looseness of his early days, the last vestiges of borrowings from Herol Graham's style, had entirely disappeared. He was more fighter than boxer, as keen to hurt as to be brilliant.

Kevin Adamson tried not to show it, but he was obviously relieved to climb down from the ring, giving way to Johnny Nelson. 'Naz is hitting as hard as any middleweight I've been in with,' said Adamson as he held out his heavy sparring gloves so that the laces could be untied. 'And Naz is much, much faster than a middleweight.' Adamson, two and a half stone heavier than Naseem, was a high-class middleweight, but he knew Naseem had his measure.

'It's become unusual for Naz to train in the afternoon,' Brendan said as he untied Adamson's laces. 'He's been training at all hours; when it suits him, really. Sometimes he comes round to the house after midnight and I open up the gym. If he's managed to get Ryan Rhodes or Johnny Nelson along, he might spar for an hour or more and then work on the pads. Then he'll sleep in until after lunch. He's a night-time person. He doesn't run any more. He doesn't need to. All the sparring he does keeps him fit. It's a different approach to training but it works. You saw him today – twenty rounds.' Brendan seemed to be trying to convince himself.

There was no need to feed Naseem with questions. He was high on himself and poured forth. 'I'm very happy with where I am,' he said. 'I've controlled everything well. I'm proud of what I've done. I'm so confident and hungry to win the world title. I can't believe the respect I've had down in London, shopping and going out at night. If I like anything, I buy it. If there is anything I desire, I'll buy it. If there's anything my stomach desires, I'll eat it.

'I've had to devote my life to boxing. It's very hard to stick at something. Guys get to sixteen or seventeen, they go out with girls, they go out drinking, smoking. Me, I live my life cleanly. I train. You haven't seen the finished product yet. I will reach my peak in my mid-twenties.

'Most people haven't got a clue about training. But I've got a winning formula for every country there is. I know how to cane the world. I've won eighteen and lost none. You've seen me sparring. I spar against cruiserweights. Sometimes, I get hit on the chin, but I don't go down. I don't think I could be overpowered unless I was out on the floor. I will never give up, no matter what weight he is, no matter how strong he is; no matter what he has won, I will be there.

'Before the age of twenty-one, I mastered the art of boxing. I owe it all to God. It's a gift from God. I've been blessed. I was the chosen one at that particular time, in 1974 when I was born. I will become a legend. I can't see myself beating myself. What's written for me is I was born to make a lot of people proud and destined to be a world champion and a legend. I can't put a limit on it, on what I can achieve, what I might earn.'

Naseem knocked out Polo Perez in the second round. He put him down first with a left hook, and again with a straight right. As Polo Perez was counted out, Naseem stood in the neutral corner, sneering and motioning with his gloves, inviting the Colombian to get to his feet to take further punishment. 'That wasn't even 50 per cent of my power,' Naseem told Sky's viewers. 'I'm not making a song and dance out of it, but believe me, they just can't take the punishment. They can't take the power. The power's extraordinary. I'm blessed by God. What can I say? It's a gift. It's early nights all the way. I'm not going the long twelve rounds, make it boring. People want excitement. They want to be entertained. I'm an entertainer, a banger and a champion too. I'm not bragging or anything, but I'm too good.'

# CHAPTER SIXTEEN

## Champion of the World

Naseem gave instructions that the women – his mother, sisters and girlfriend – must not be at ringside at the Cardiff rugby stadium when he tore the world featherweight title from the grasp of Steve Robinson on the last day of September 1995. The atmosphere was going to be evil. And so was Naseem.

In the away team's changing room under the main stand, Naseem and his entourage could hear the crowd preparing to receive them. Through the filthy evening, as the rain fell steadily and the fighters on the undercard performed to scant attention, swelling chants of 'Steve-O, Steve-O' had broken out around the huge bowl of the stadium, echoing and spreading in waves. As Brendan carefully bandaged and taped Naseem's hands, the chants reached a focused intensity. 'Hamed, Hamed, who the fuck is Hamed?'

There was tension in the room. Jon Thaxton, who had been Naseem's principal sparring partner for the fight, sat on a bench against the wall. Thaxton was a tough, stocky, fair-haired and determined fighter from Norwich, who had been under Brendan's wing for a few years. His job was to help protect Naseem as he made his way through the crowd to the ring, and he wasn't looking forward to it. As for the fight itself, Jon Thaxton wasn't nervous for Naseem. He knew all too well what he could do. But he was nervous for Brendan: he understood how much it meant, how awful it would be for Brendan if anything went wrong. Brendan was nervous for Brendan, too, wondering whether this would finally be the night when he could say he had trained a world champion.

Naseem smiled. He was never nervous and a world title fight, the night of destiny, was no exception. He wanted it all against him. He wanted hostility. At every opportunity for months, and especially in the last week before the fight, Naseem had been deliberately and systematically belittling Robinson. He did it partly to upset Robinson, but also to invite hatred from Robinson's supporters, to swim in poison. Somehow, the odds against him were not enough. It meant nothing to Naseem that many boxing experts predicted that Robinson's experience – eight world title fights, all won – would be significant. He couldn't care less that in his first fight as a featherweight, the nine-stone limit, he was taking on a man who had long campaigned in that division and who was considered the strongest physically of all featherweights. To really fight, to commit himself completely, Naseem needed to sense danger. He needed to take on Robinson's army as well as Robinson himself.

As usual, the most relaxed person in the dressing room was Naseem. He had been dancing before his hands were taped, and he resumed when Brendan had finished, pausing only to speak towards a hand-held television camera. Was he worried about the crowd? he was asked. 'They can shout as loud as they want,' Naseem said. 'It's going to give me a better buzz.'

Naseem's entrance was via a ramp, built with steel scaffolding poles and stretching from high in the stand down to ground level. The lights went down, a flare was ignited at the top of the ramp and as the yellow smoke dispersed in the damp night air, the figure of Naseem was revealed. He was dressed in a slightly less flamboyant fashion, wearing a white poncho, but he danced in his usual manner as he made his way down. On the ramp, he was high above the crowd, safe. At the bottom, where his escort – Brendan, John Ingle, Ryan Rhodes, Jon Thaxton and his brothers Riath and Nabeel – waited, he was vulnerable. The hatred was closing in. A couple of the boyos tried to climb over the crowd-control barriers to get at Naseem. Stewards pushed them back. The chanting was all around the stadium, but face to face, personal, as well. 'Hamed, Hamed, who the hell is Hamed?' and 'Bastard, Paki bastard', the refrain from Naseem's childhood.

And they spat, spittle settling on the hair and shoulders of Naseem and his guardians. Naseem stopped by the steps leading to the ring and was hit on the side of his head by a coin. He rubbed the spot, stepped up to the ring-apron, stood for a moment with his gloves on the top rope and sprang into a front flip, over the rope, landing feet first on the canvas to jeers of derision. The poncho had draped itself over his head. He shook his head until it fell free and stood stock still, looking to left and right, his jaw tilted in defiance.

As champion, Robinson was second to the ring, entering down the same ramp and to an equally loud but very different reception. He ducked through the ropes in the conventional way and acknowledged his supporters by bowing his head and raising his left hand. When he lifted his head, his face wore a hollow, apologetic expression. He must have known.

They both knew. For years, Naseem had been planning to beat opponents mentally. 'When I come up against the good kids, the really good fighters, I know I'm going to have to beat them mentally, to do their heads in,' he said soon after turning professional. Over the years, going to the fights around the country with Brendan, he had seen fighters lose in dressing rooms, weigh-ins, even press conferences, almost as often as he had seen them lose in the ring. He knew that when Mike Tyson appeared invincible, his opponents were beaten long before he laid a glove on them. He knew that when Muhammad Ali, in the days when he was Cassius Clay, had taunted Sonny Liston, seeking him out in public places, calling him 'a great ugly bear', it was to sow doubt and confusion.

Naseem had grasped the power of psychology in boxing. One of the mind games might be called Beating the Contradiction. The contradiction is fighting a man you don't know, whom you don't hate, with whom you have much in common, and with whom you have no argument. To fight without hate or argument is unnatural and empty. The trick is to invent the argument, to imagine the slight. That is why the hype before a big fight is contrived, but, for the fighters, often necessary. Marvin Hagler, the great middleweight, used to find it next to impossible even to train properly until he knew the name of his opponent. Once he knew it, he went to work. As he ran, sparred and did his exercises, he intoned his opponent's name like a mantra, tuning himself to a perfect pitch of hatred. In 1984 Hagler fought the British middleweight, Tony Sibson, in Worcester, Massachusetts. It was Sibson's first trip to America and he was wide-eyed and touched by the welcome until, at a press conference, he met Hagler. Sibson, a cheery, genial man, said hello and put his hand on Hagler's shoulder. Hagler, who had been mumbling 'Sibson, Sibson' for three months as he put his body through torture, turned and glared. 'Touch me again and I'll drop you right here.' Sibson recoiled, already beaten.

The quick-witted bully is the worst, and Naseem never missed a trick as he set about the needling of Robinson. It wasn't difficult, for Robinson was a hard, honest fighter, the kind of whom it is said that he had paid his dues. Success had come late to him, and somewhat surprisingly. He was a journeyman with a good but unexceptional record until he was called up at short notice as a substitute when Ruben Palacio, a Colombian world champion fighting in Britain, tested positive for HIV. Robinson grabbed his chance, defeating John Davison on points for the vacant title in April 1993. For two and half years he defended his title against one fancied contender after another, beating them all.

One of Naseem's attempts at psychological disruption did not work at all. Mindful of the famous occasion when Cassius Clay visited Sonny Liston's house with a bear-trap, Naseem and friends set off from his hotel near Newport late one night, a few days before the fight. The idea was to disturb Robinson's beauty sleep, and they headed for his house in two cars rigged with super-loud audio systems. On the motorway, the lead car had a puncture and both cars pulled on to the hard shoulder. The police arrived and asked all occupants to get out of the cars. It was raining and Naseem sat tight in the back of the second car, flanked by John Ingle and Steve Bunce, a boxing journalist. They wound down their windows a little, but it was getting awkward; the police still wanted everyone outside. Steve Bunce tried diplomacy, telling the police that Naseem was fighting for a world title in Cardiff and he mustn't catch cold. It worked: the police relented and left. Once the flat tyre had been changed, the cars headed back to the hotel.

Naseem's other tactics were more effective. At one press conference, a few days before the fight, Naseem's entourage wore T-shirts with the slogan NASEEM HAMED, WORLD CHAMPION. Robinson's trainer complained at the presumption and Naseem said he wasn't going to get T-shirts printed with the word 'Contender' on them and then have to change them all after the fight. The press conference was one-sided and Naseem made sure Robinson knew it. 'Come on,' he said after fielding a stream of questions; 'ask Steve some questions. He's world champion after all, until Saturday.' But poor Steve, struck dumb like Liston used to be when Cassius Clay was in full flow, had little to say.

But Naseem's most killing blow outside the ring was at the final press conference at the Cardiff International Arena two days before the fight. He spotted Robinson waiting by a door while Frank Warren was being interviewed by a television journalist. Naseem moved in immediately.

'What's up, Steve?'

'Oh, I'm waiting to see Frank.'

'Are you going to see him to ask for more money?'

'I'm waiting to see Frank.'

'If you want more money, Steve, I'll bet my purse against yours. And if you think I'm getting a million pounds for boxing you, and you're not, and you think you should be getting more, it's a good gamble. Let's fight for winner takes all, put all the money in one pot. Frank's in there. Let's get him not to make out two cheques but just one and to fill in the winner's name after the fight. How about it, Steve?'

'I'll have to talk to my lawyer.'

'No Steve, we're not on about lawyers, or managers. Your money against my money. If you're a man and you're one hundred per cent confident of your ability to beat me like you've said all along, and that I'm just a blown-up super-bantamweight, and you'll be too strong, and you're the best featherweight in the world, then put your money on the line.'

Steve Robinson muttered again about seeing his lawyer, but Naseem had looked into Robinson's eyes and had seen what he wanted. At that moment they both knew, and when Robinson joined Naseem in the ring they both knew. Because Robinson knew, the crowd's roaring, blind support embarrassed him. He knew he would let them down. Because Naseem knew, the crowd's hatred heightened his pleasure.

Naseem had decided to dispense with the usual opening phase, the exploration. When the first bell sounded, he went straight in on Robinson and opened up with both hands, wide to the body around the sides of Robinson's guard. Immediately, the unvarying pattern of the fight was established: Robinson holding his gloves high, his elbows tucked in, protecting his head and the front of his upper body; Naseem standing in front of him, waiting for a glimpse of an opening to fire a punch through the guard, meanwhile throwing wide punches to hit the belly and the side of Robinson's torso, which were unprotected. The contrast in posture could not have been more marked. Robinson, hiding behind his exaggerated defence, could only shuffle forward, or swing round on his axis, like a dalek. With Robinson in front of him almost static, Naseem, his hands held low, often dangling by his waist, his shoulders relaxed, enjoyed free range. He could stand square on, he could dance. He could even, he discovered, face Robinson at close -quarters, keep his hands low and offer his chin as a target. In that first round of his first world title fight, he stuck out his chin like a gnome and tapped it with his glove: there you are Steve Robinson, have a pop at that, if you dare.

When an opponent offers such an invitation, intended to demean, there are three choices: try to hit the chin and succeed, which is fine; try to hit the chin and fail, which is humiliating; or ignore it. Robinson ignored it, probably the best option. In any case, his most pressing problem was that the fortress tactic was proving worse than useless. Mostly, Robinson stayed behind the ramparts while Naseem blew holes in his lower walls as he pleased. And when Robinson summoned the nerve to emerge on a sortie, he immediately suffered damage to the upper parts.

The medieval defence may not have been Robinson's original intention. Several of those watching close at ringside, including Jon Thaxton, Naseem's sparring partner, and Frank Warren, believed that Robinson was hurt badly very early in the fight. It could have been one of those first two shots that Naseem threw in his furious introduction.

94

Whenever it was, it was at that moment that Robinson experienced the shock that faces every opponent of Naseem. His speed is expected, for every boxer among the lighter weights has to be fast, and a very good man among the lightweights is likely to be very fast. But they cannot believe how hard he hits. It is quite beyond their experience that a man of nine stone or less can hit with such power. The first hit produces a reflex reaction: pain. But it also brings a dreadful realisation. Every plan, every best hope is dissolved, to be replaced by the most basic instinct, survival.

Those who box regularly with Naseem, Jon Thaxton for example, learn in time to cope with the speed, the power, the unexpected sequences of blows, the peculiar angles. It helps that they have also learned Brendan's footwork, the switch-hitting and the combinations. After a few sessions, they find a way to anticipate the worst damage and avoid it. They even hand something out in return. But to encounter Naseem for the first time when it really matters, in a public fight, is a terrible ordeal. Even though Robinson felt doomed as he entered the ring, he clung to one conviction: that he would be the stronger man, the bigger puncher. He was a natural featherweight, indeed he was exceptionally strong for a featherweight, and Naseem, shorter and less muscular, less tough-looking, had never even fought a featherweight. When that single comfort had gone, Robinson was left with no prospect but to be hurt and hurt again until he dropped – to be Naseem's punch-bag.

Robinson suffered many humiliations. Naseem was talking to him and laughing from the beginning. Naseem stood still with his hands below his waist, wobbled his shoulders and rocked his head from side to side like a string-puppet. He waggled his hips and put his left hand high in the air as if waving through a crowd to a friend. This had nothing and everything to do with boxing. It was an assertion of contempt but also a demonstration that Naseem could take any risk because there was no likelihood of being hit. Naseem, dangling and laughing, and Robinson, grimly taking no notice and staying tight behind his defence, presented an extreme contrast. One was tense and rigid; the other relaxed, liquid.

In the third round, Robinson summoned an attack. It was a matter of close-your-eyes-hit-and-hope. He went after Naseem and threw twelve consecutive punches at Naseem's head. In isolation, it would have looked impressive, for they were sharp punches and the combinations of jabs and hooks were well constructed. It impressed spectators, especially those too far from the ring to tell the difference between a punch that nearly hits and a punch that really hits. But every one of them missed the target. Naseem moved this way and that, slipping one, ducking the next, until number twelve whistled past. While the attack was progressing, Naseem had not attempted a counter, as if he was interested to see what Robinson had to offer. But once the flurry was over, Naseem produced the punctuation, a single, short, stinging left-hand punch that found its mark on the right side of Robinson's head. Naseem laughed again.

In the fourth round, Naseem mimicked Muhammad Ali with a sudden shuffle and double shuffle of his feet, and by circling easily to his right and snaking out the right-hand lead. It is a punch that can look languid and obvious, but also inevitable, like a harpoon on its way to the whale. It was a round not of fighting but display and when it ended, Naseem placed himself between Robinson and Robinson's corner, put his gloves on his hips so that his elbows stood out, opened his eyes wide and performed a hula-hula.

There is always the fear, especially among those watching, that one punch can turn and drain the strongest tide. Brendan in particular would never forget what had happened to Herol Graham against Julian Jackson. But there were others, including Frank Warren and Jon Thaxton, both close enough to touch the canvas, who were anxious that Naseem should do what was so obviously within his power – stop playing with Robinson and hurt him so badly as to remove his last trace of hope. Naseem obliged in the fifth. It started with a punch, a left hook in mid-ring, that was no harder than most of its predecessors but that found its way through Robinson's two-handed guard and cracked him on the chin. For a moment, both fighters took stock. It was an intimate moment in that both knew what no one else knew. Robinson was badly hurt. He hadn't staggered or winced, but his eyes betrayed him. And they both knew what would happen next. Robinson remained with his hands in front of his face, covered up. Naseem opened his eyes and his mouth, grinning, salivating, the pleasure of anticipation flooding his senses, the sadist approaching orgasm. He planted his feet to set his stance, and tightened his face for the effort ahead. Every punch now would be full power. Left hook first. It impacted high on Robinson's head. The right hook was already on its way. It caught Robinson on the glove but with such force that his upper body was twisted sharply to his right. On its way, his face met the decisive punch, another left hook that crashed into Robinson's chin and detached his senses. He fell to his left, avoiding the worst of the right uppercut that was the fourth and final punch of the attack, and crumpled on to the canvas. Naseem's face had relaxed into a sneer as he watched him fall. He raised his arms in triumph, and then moved forward, wanting to stand over his fallen opponent. The referee held him back as Robinson clambered to his feet and looked forlornly towards his corner.

'Box on!'

Robinson's pride remained intact. He managed to survive the remainder of the round as Naseem pursued him, but the effect of Naseem's punches was revealed. Robinson's face was swollen, the flesh around his eyes puffy so that he was peering through slits.

The issue was beyond chance, what the chroniclers of Regency prize fighting calculated as 'all Lombard Street to a china orange', but Robinson's supporters made a last effort to encourage their man. In the sixth round, when Naseem had reverted to casual command, biding his time, a chanting chorus was taken up around the stadium: 'Rob-in-son, Rob-in-son, Rob-in-son'. Even at bay, desperately tired and hurting, the kill imminent, Robinson heard the simple, insistent rhythm of the chant. And he might have drawn comfort, even strength, from the message that the massed ranks of his countrymen still believed. But his tormentor seized the chant for his own purpose. First, Naseem sang 'Rob-in-son, Rob-in-son' himself. Then he delivered the ultimate humiliation. He sang and punched in unison, 'Rob-in-son, Rob-in-son', left, right, left, one straight punch for every syllable.

As he sat on his stool in the corner during the interval between the seventh and eighth rounds, Naseem told Brendan: 'I'm going to dummy him and drop him with the left hook.'

The end had an air of unreality, of anticlimax. But for all, it was a relief. Naseem hunted for the first minute and a half of the eighth round from the southpaw stance. He threw a few long punches by way of exploration. He was serious, looking intently for the opening. As he circled to his left, he switched to the orthodox stance. He dipped slightly and gave just a suggestion of a right-hand lead, no more than a twitch. It was the dummy, but there was no indication that Robinson realised. He had merely seen Naseem closing on him and pawed out his right hand to keep him away. The gesture was irrelevant. Naseem, standing square, turned to his right and threw one punch. If there is a valid distinction between the speed and power of a punch, this was a fast one, a clip. It landed around Robinson's right ear and had an effect quite out of proportion to its apparent weight. Robinson appeared to leap backwards, but in an extraordinary way. His left leg bent at the knee, ready for the landing, but his right leg was stiff, and sliding behind him. He had not only lost balance, but had lost function, a giraffe on marbles.

By the time the desperate dance had become a fall, Robinson was horizontal. He met the canvas with a single thump as if he had been dropped unconscious from a height. He tried to stand but the referee wanted no further evidence. He waved his arms to signal the end of the fight and to pronounce Naseem world champion.

For the first interview, before the sweat had dried, before the passion of the fight had subsided, Naseem sat on the ring-apron, leaning against the ropes, the championship belt slung over his left shoulder. Brendan knelt behind him, on the other side of the ropes.

'I'm not making a big song and dance about it,' Naseem said, employing what had become a favourite phrase as he looked directly at the television camera. 'You've seen it for yourself. I'm world champion. The belt's there. The viewers know who's the best. He said he was too strong. What happened? I was too strong, too fast, too good, and I'm world champion.'

'Let's have a word for Brendan,' said the interviewer. 'He's had you for a long time and he's made you what you are. Give him some credit.'

Naseem was looking to his left, away from Brendan. There was a sense of awkwardness, of confirmation refused. Brendan ended it by speaking himself.

'He done the job.'

'Great credit,' said Naseem at last. But he was still looking away.

'I'm over the moon for him,' said Brendan. He bent down and, uninvited, kissed Naseem on the top of the head.

# CHAPTER SEVENTEEN
## The Gypsy's Warning

It arrived unannounced, evil on the fairest day. Naseem saw the left lead as the cherry-red glove spat snakelike towards him. He stood his ground and ducked low to his right, the limbo defence. The punch passed harmlessly over his left shoulder, and Naseem prepared for the counter. Make them miss, make them pay. He came out of the crouch, left hand loaded, ready to fire, standing up, target located, rocket on its way, and, crash! He had been hit with the right, hadn't seen it, he was falling into the underworld, his legs useless, his right hand paddling, trying to break the fall, and, bang! He hit the canvas.

Only once before in his life had Naseem been knocked down. It happened in Brendan's gym, a few years earlier. Naseem was sparring with Adam Fogerty, a useful heavyweight, six foot four, sixteen and a half stone, and, as usual with Naseem, the bigger man was missing, being made to look an idiot. Then Fogerty got lucky. He closed his eyes, guessed, and aimed a punch at the air. It arrived in a place momentarily occupied by Naseem's chin. Down went Naseem, landing on his back but bouncing straight back on to his feet, as if from a trampoline. He tore into Fogerty, knocking him around the ring, punishing him, wreaking vengeance. They had to pull him off.

Now the indignity was painfully public. Naseem had been knocked down at the Newcastle Arena in the third minute of the first round of his second defence of the world featherweight title. And it wasn't only the live audience, or the viewers on Sky who witnessed Naseem's fall. For the first time, Naseem was being introduced to the American public, the ultimate source of wealth in boxing. Ten million viewers of Showtime, the subscription channel which had a long-term contract with Don King, the partner of Frank Warren, had the pleasure of seeing the bragging sensation from England brought low. No one could deny it was poetic justice, for a few minutes earlier Naseem had entered the arena borne like Cleopatra on a burnish'd throne, supported by eight black shaven-headed men representing Nubian slaves. He had dismounted and jiggled to the ring on a path strewn with rose petals. No wonder spectators and viewers were amused as well as surprised when they saw him dumped on the canvas.

For some time, Naseem, who seemed to have forgotten the Fogerty incident, had boasted that he would never be knocked down, that such a proposition was ludicrous. But Daniel Alicea, a twenty-three-year-old Puerto Rican who had been a brilliant amateur, and who had achieved enough in his fifteen professional contests to be nominated as the unbeaten, number one challenger for Naseem's world title, obviously had another view.

Alicea had come to fight and knew how to fight, which was more than could be said for Naseem's opponent in his first world title defence, the hand-picked, unfortunate Said Lawal. Lawal had a very strange background for a boxer. He was a Nigerian based in Vienna. But somehow that seemed in keeping, for the fight, which was held in a conference centre in Glasgow, was one leg of a gargantuan, Gothic triple-header programme with which Sky launched pay-per-view television in Britain. Subscribers to Sky had to pay an extra £9.95 for the dubious privilege of watching Frank Bruno against Mike Tyson in Las Vegas (Bruno froze); ancient Joe Bugner against Scott Welch in Berlin (Bugner congealed); and Naseem against Lawal, who was petrified. Lawal was knocked down by the first punch Naseem threw and was saved by the referee after thirty-five seconds, the fifth shortest world title fight in history. Lawal, whose nose was broken in two places, subsequently asked his seconds what time he was due to go on.

If that absurdly easy win made Naseem complacent, the reports from Alicea's training camp made him worse. When Alicea arrived in Newcastle, he was short of sparring partners. Frank Warren arranged for Paul Griffin, an Irish featherweight trained by Brendan, to help out. As an amateur, Griffin had been a European champion (and therefore a successor to Brendan's brother, Jimmy), ranked number two in the world. He had lost only twelve of 270 amateur contests. A dark-haired, intense fighter, he was clever but very orthodox and when he turned professional at the late age of twenty-three, he found it difficult to adapt to Brendan's training methods. When he sparred with Naseem, Griffin was given a horrible time, partly because he was a newcomer to the gym, an invader, partly because of his amateur credentials, partly because he was a fellow featherweight, and mostly because in sparring Naseem gave everyone a horrible time.

Griffin was in awe of Naseem's boxing: 'I've never experienced anything like his power. There's times he's hit me and I thought he's hit me with a hammer. He does a whip shot with the right and it's like a smack with an iron bar. If he hits anyone on the chin, from nine stone to eleven stone, they're gone. When he's fighting I always look at his opponent, at the guy's face. When he gets hit, it's like he thinks he's been hit by a truck.'

Griffin went to Newcastle as requested and had one sparring session of four rounds and two sessions of five rounds with Alicea, and he hammered him. Griffin was the only person who had boxed both with Naseem and with Alicea, the champion and the challenger. He was the best-placed man in the world to judge the fight.

When Naseem arrived in Newcastle, he said to Griffin in the hotel: 'What's he like?'

'He's a strong kid,' said Griffin. 'But you're going to knock him out.'

Frank Warren also bumped into Griffin before the fight. He had some anxiety about Alicea, knowing him to be an improving fighter of substantial potential. Indeed, it was Warren's idea for Naseem to dispose of Alicea early in the piece rather than take him on in a couple of years' time, when he might be more dangerous.

Warren asked the same question as Naseem: 'What's he like?'

'Nothing special,' said Griffin.

But once the fight itself was under way, it didn't take long for Alicea to prove he knew enough to take advantage of any holes in Naseem's defence. And there were holes, because Naseem had begun to discard patience and care in favour of his latest toy, the power-punch that he called his rocket-launcher. Three times, Alicea caught Naseem with a right during that first round. The third, the knockdown, was a classic, the trickster tricked: Alicea led with the left, let Naseem counter, but beat him to it, countering the counter.

Alicea caught him, and Naseem tumbled, but he was more embarrassed than hurt. The right hand he had flung out on his airborne journey had cushioned the fall and his head never hit the canvas. He was up immediately, took the standing count of eight required by the rules, and was ready to resume. Naseem shook his head not so much to show he wasn't hurt as to deny it had really happened. At ringside, Frank Warren, no doubt conscious of the investment implications of defeat, had turned a ghastly pale. Naseem's father and brothers gasped. Brendan, in the corner, was thinking, serve him right, now maybe he'll listen. The reason he had always said that Naseem might beat himself one day, was to try to stop it happening. But now Brendan also wanted to see Naseem taught the lesson of neglecting training, of knowing it all. As soon as he allowed himself that heretical thought, however, it was superseded by a stronger, opposite determination. If Naseem was undone, those who would have the most satisfaction would be the doubters, the managers, pundits and journalists who had ignored or ridiculed Naseem and Brendan from the beginning. That was a prospect Brendan could not bear. Naseem had to win.

The bell rang for the end of the first round. Naseem sat on his stool and for the first time in his life admitted he had a problem in the ring. When Brendan removed the gumshield from his mouth, Naseem said: 'What do I do now?'

Now you want to know, thought Brendan. 'Right,' he said. 'Tuck up and walk to him, jab and then use your combinations off the jab.'

The fears of Warren and Naseem's family, the confused emotions of Brendan, and the pleasure of the doubters, were all short-lived. The doubters, in any case, had it all wrong. Their distaste for anything unmanly, fancy, lured them into the fallacy that the disco boxer is effeminate. It's all very well, they said, but Hamed won't be able to dance and hold his hands down by his waist when he faces a top man. He'll get hit then, and can he take a shot? And if he gets hurt, has he got the heart, the bottle? Those who had seen Naseem on the few occasions he had been hurt in the gym, and especially those who had done it, knew the answer. Naseem might be a bully, but he was no coward. He would die rather than yield. Once, he had told Brendan: 'You must never pull me out of a fight. Never. Or you're sacked straight away.' The point was not what might happen to Naseem if he was hurt, but God help the man who did it.

Like Fogerty, Alicea was soon to regret his temerity. Before the second round had been completed, he had been hurt, knocked down and finally dispatched with a combination more complex and far more deadly than the one with which he had caught Naseem. Each element of the sequence found Alicea's head: the left uppercut twisting his face one way; to be met by the right cross to force it back; only to collide with another opposing force, the left uppercut again. Alicea did not so much fall as melt. His head hit the canvas with the thump that worries the brain surgeon, and the referee, realising that a count was futile, rushed to his aid, wrenching the gumshield from his mouth.

Naseem made light of his own brief acquaintance with the canvas. 'I went down and tested it for him,' he said. 'I predicted I would take him out in two rounds, and I did.' Brendan smiled for the cameras. But once they reached the dressing room, he told Naseem: 'To get hit with the right is bad. To get hit twice with the right is terrible. To get hit with it three times is suicidal.'

That was the first warning, what Brendan called the gypsy's warning. The second was just around the corner. It could hardly have been more different, for if the first warning was a shock, sudden in its arrival and departure, the second warning was prolonged torture.

The opponent for Naseem's third defence of the world title two months later was by far the most dangerous man he had met. In boxing parlance, Mexicans come in two categories: road-sweepers and assassins. Manuel Medina, who had twice held a version of the world featherweight title, was very much the latter. Naseem's preparations could hardly have been worse. As the fight approached, he had problems with weight. It wasn't that he couldn't make the nine-stone featherweight limit, but that he was training to get the weight off, rather than getting to the weight and then training for the contest.

Brendan had conceded control. Forced to choose between resigning with his pride intact and accepting a subservient role, he had given in to Naseem on training matters, as he had given in to him over money. Arguments about money and percentages had poisoned their relationship and it didn't help that Brendan had to accept that he had in effect become Naseem's employee.

Brendan could no longer pretend to himself that Naseem could get away with ignoring the fundamentals of training, that he was different from every fighter that had gone before him, that he was a night person and that sparring was by itself sufficient preparation. He could see that Naseem's timing was out, his mobility reduced, his conditioning imperfect. In sparring, it was noticeable that he was having problems with Johnny Nelson and Ryan Rhodes, whom he used to handle without difficulty. But although Naseem could no longer claim he would never be knocked down, his belief that he could not be beaten had been perversely reinforced by the Alicea fight. His constant refrain was that he had been chosen by God, the provider of his talent, the supplier of the rocket-launcher that would always see him through.

The fight was on a Saturday night, 31 August 1996, in Dublin. On the Tuesday before, Naseem and his entourage, which seemed to expand with every fight, toured the city on an open-top bus. Perhaps that was where he caught a cold. In the steam room of the country house hotel outside Dublin, Naseem coughed phlegm, spitting it into the metal grate on the floor. The driver assigned to him was sent to buy some medicine. Frank Warren found out and stopped Naseem taking it. He could have failed the drugs test after the fight. Instead, Warren called a doctor, who prescribed antibiotics. Brendan and Warren, and Naseem's brother, Riath, all urged him to pull out of the fight, to have it postponed for three weeks. But Naseem, who was still coughing up phlegm in the car on the way to the fight, insisted on going ahead. His public was waiting and the rocket-launcher would suffice.

It almost did. He came out blazing and caught Medina late in the second round. Medina did well to beat the count, and even better to remain upright, with his legs wobbling, until the bell.

But when Naseem returned to his corner for the minute's rest between rounds, he was in trouble himself. Exhausted, he was fighting for breath. When he went out for the third, he could hardly hold up his hands. For several rounds, Naseem did little more than survive. The defensive skills learned by every boxer taught by Brendan, that will-o'-the-wisp art of avoidance, had deserted him. Physically weak, his timing absent, his speed reduced, unbalanced, he was discovering what a fight is like for an ordinary boxer – hard and cruel. Naseem lunged in vain at Medina and was forced to take hurtful punches. In each round, he prayed for the bell to sound for rest and relief from the pain. In the eighth, Medina ducked underneath a Naseem lead and brought his right hand over the top, catching Naseem flush on the mouth. Naseem did not fall, but his gumshield flew across the ring as if expelled from a catapult.

Through unaccustomed adversity, Naseem kept fighting, kept believing. He began to make headway, to hold his own and to inflict some damage on Medina. It became a desperate struggle between tired men, a battle of wills. At last, moments before the end of the eleventh round, Medina's seconds surprisingly threw in the towel. Their man had been beaten to a standstill. Naseem's hardest fight was won.

'From the second to the sixth rounds, I don't know how he fought,' said Brendan. 'He had nothing to fight with. From the sixth to the eleventh, it was unbelievable. I'd given up worrying in the corner. I was just thinking that you pay to learn, that he had brought it all on himself. So I just enjoyed watching him struggle.'

Afterwards, Naseem and Brendan were walking through the arena towards the room where the press conference was to be held. Naseem was shattered, but he said to Brendan: 'You didn't think I was going to get beat, did you?'

'No,' said Brendan. 'But I got great pleasure from watching you struggle. You've gone higher, sky high in my estimation. It was like Ali against Frazier, the thriller in Manila. Your body was sick. You were on antibiotics. You could have died in there. But what can you do when you won't listen? You're sore now. Tomorrow, you'll be in pain.

You won't know whether you're coming or going. You'll have aches and pains for days.'

'Yes,' said Naseem. 'But I won, didn't I?'

Hard as it had been for Naseem, it was infinitely harder for Medina. At the press conference, his face was in a shocking state, and it was obvious that his handlers had been right to pull him out, even though there were only a few seconds left of the eleventh round. If they had let him continue, he might never have fought again.

Naseem was asked what he had learned. 'I learned that if you have a cold a few days before a fight, you don't box,' he said. And he concluded: 'In my mind, I can't get beat. I just cannot get beat.'

# CHAPTER EIGHTEEN
## Gates Fit For Versailles

A visit to Brendan's gym used to be a reminder of the constants of life. It was bound to be raining; Newman Road would be granite-grey and depressing; but the heavy black door was always open, like churches used to be, the paint on the walls was still peeling and furred with damp, the smell a sweaty perfume both nauseating and enticing, the scene within timeless: boxers ploughing up and down the lines, others sparring in the ring, and Brendan sitting on his steps. But one afternoon in the early days of January 1997, a few weeks before Naseem fought Tom Johnson, it was immediately obvious that the place had changed. Superficially, perhaps, it was a sign of progress. But for those romantically attached to the old hall, it was a kind of desecration.

The culprit was success. Outside the gym was one of Naseem's motors, a Porsche Carrera, registration number NAZ 1. Inside, the ring posts and girders had been plastered with Adidas advertisements. These days, you were as likely to encounter a film crew as a mother or social worker with a tearaway in tow, and someone had decided that every advertising advantage must be taken.

But these were minor alterations compared with Brendan's gates. At the entrance to the yard outside Brendan's house, a pair of black gates had been erected. These were no ordinary gates. They were wrought iron, massive, grandiose, supported by a huge arch, with spikes and flourishes, mostly painted black, but the spikes and flourishes in gold – gates fit for Versailles.

In Versailles, they had a phrase for gates that were out of place and proportion: *la folie des grandeurs*. In Wincobank, they used expressions that were more down to earth. But for Brendan, the gates were more important than people knew. He had decided on them after Naseem won the world title. He asked Steven Hinchcliffe, a friend whose business was wrought iron, to bring down some designs. Brendan picked out the best gates to be had, along with the flourishes, spikes and curls. He dug the holes himself. It took two days; working from eight until five, he used a sledgehammer, crowbar and shovel to get through three feet of concrete. Steven Hinchcliffe arrived with two assistants, plus the gates. It took a day to assemble the gates and several days for a painter to make them gleam, black and gold. All told, they cost more than £3,000. When Alma saw them, she nearly died. She couldn't believe how big they were. Brendan wasn't around, so she tackled Steven Hinchcliffe who said they had to be that size, and that you had to have a big arch over the top to support the gates. You couldn't do them any smaller. It was not an argument that Alma found entirely convincing, and she interrogated Brendan when he came home. His explanation was that everyone around Wincobank complained about the articles in the papers which said the gym was in a run-down area, and that it brought the value of the houses down, so he thought he'd do his bit to improve the neighbourhood, and anyway, he liked the gates. What Brendan didn't say was that the gates were a symbol and a statement. It might be a clumsy statement. It might be over the top, and the gates were certainly out of place in Newman Road, but they were his way of saying: 'I've made something of myself. I've achieved something.'

Naseem said the gates were too big. They were ridiculous. Brendan didn't seem to mind, because the New Year had revealed a new Naseem. He was taking his next fight, against another reigning world champion, Tom Johnson, seriously, training flat out; in fact training properly for the first time since he prepared to go twelve rounds with Belcastro.

In the gym, Naseem, in devastating form, was bashing up Jon Thaxton. They sparred for ten rounds before Thaxton dragged his body from the ring. Thaxton was one of the best ten-stone men in Europe. Born in Norfolk of Anglo-Saxon stock, bullish and unconquerably tough, he was the fittest man in the gym and the most determined. But as Thaxton was brave, taking shots and still coming on, firing back, so was Naseem brilliant. Against Thaxton he had to be, and not just in bursts, but for three minutes of every round.

After Christmas, while Brendan had been putting up his gates, Naseem had flown across the Atlantic in Concorde to film an advertisement for Adidas, the sportswear company with which he had just signed a ten-fight sponsorship deal worth a reported £4 million. The ad, shot in black and white, opened with a shot of a New York skyscraper. On the roof, a wild-haired prophet shrieked a warning to the citizens below: 'You will salute him. You will fall before him. You will listen to what he has to say. He will not be defeated. Hear the wise man, America!' Naseem was shown training in a gym and packing a kitbag on board a ship. He went up on deck, somersaulted the railings as if they were ropes round a ring, and landed on the dockside. The prophet screamed: 'You're too late. He's already here. He is here. Prince Naseem, here on business.'

Except that he wasn't there. Naseem, for the moment, remained an unknown in New York and the advertisement was perhaps a prediction, perhaps wishful thinking. That was one reason Naseem took the Johnson fight so seriously. Johnson represented another step up in class and at least another magnification in public exposure. The holder of the International Boxing Federation's version of the world featherweight title for four years, Johnson had made eleven successful defences, and was regarded in American boxing circles as the most accomplished man at the weight.

After the ten rounds with Jon Thaxton, Naseem went five equally vigorous rounds with Johnny Nelson, showered and changed before taking off in the Porsche. Later that evening, in the steam room of the leisure centre attached to the most expensive hotel in Sheffield, Naseem lay face down on a bench while Brendan massaged his legs with an oily mixture made to his own recipe. It was so hot it was hard to speak or think. Pores ran like sluices and brains were surely being poached, but Naseem was used to it, for a session in the steam had long been a part of his after-training routine.

Naseem was in Napoleonic mood. Even in private, when he spoke softly, he issued statements. The result was not so much a conversation as a one-to-one press conference. 'Johnson's good, but he's made for me. I'll take him in the third round. I usually prefer the second, but this time my mum says it'll be the third, so the third it's going to be. I'm running again. Every morning I'm up at five and running in the dark. I'm fitter and stronger than ever before. I gave up roadwork because I hated it, but this time I've stuck with it and it's helped my legs and my breathing. Tonight I sparred fifteen rounds and at the end of it I was still fresh.'

Brendan chimed in, rubbing away and purring. 'He's been marvellous. He's living right and training right. He knows that the only one who can beat him is himself. He's learned the lesson. He knows he should never have gone in against Medina with that cold. His chest was terrible and he couldn't breathe. He could hardly hold up his hands. That could have been fifteen years' work down the drain.'

'I couldn't wait for the bell,' said Naseem, casting aside the imperial manner and admitting to vulnerability in the ring. 'I was so tired, I was gone, every round after the second.' He paused. 'But I still beat him up.'

After the massage, in the changing room, Brendan showed Naseem a fax he had been sent. It was a copy of an article that Sheffield's local paper, the *Star*, intended to run. A woman had made a complaint that Naseem had parked in a disabled bay at the Meadowhall shopping centre and that when she confronted him, he had been abusive.

'That's rubbish,' said Naseem. 'If I did park there it was by mistake and it was ten o'clock at night anyway. There were loads of disabled bays and they were all empty.'

'Yes, but it's bad press,' said Brendan. 'Why not make a statement saying it was a mistake, apologise to the lady and make a donation to charity? Then you can turn it into good publicity.'

'I'm not talking to that paper. Finish.'

The *Star* had covered Naseem's career from the beginning, from his first amateur fight at the Cutler's Hall. But recently they had carried adverse publicity, including reports of Naseem's court appearances for driving offences, and he had decided to withdraw cooperation. 'You can't censor the press,' Brendan said. But Naseem was immovable.

With the Johnson fight three weeks away, that was the only fly in the ointment. Brendan could hardly contain his pleasure that Naseem had again dedicated himself to training. His faith had been renewed: Naseem could yet be the perfect fighter, could avoid beating himself, could be better than Ali, could reach his potential, and could prove to the sceptics that Brendan's system worked.

For Naseem, all was set fair. His fortune was assured by the twin pillars of Sky and Adidas. Along with his parents, brothers and sisters, he had finally left the shop in Newman Road. He had bought two houses side by side for his family, and another, which had belonged to Trevor Francis when he was manager of Sheffield Wednesday, for himself. His collection of cars was growing, and included a Mercedes given to him by the President of the Yemen. His eldest brother, Riath, had become his commercial manager. Nabeel was running the official fan club. Two companies, Naseem Hamed Enterprises Ltd and Naseem Hamed Promotions Ltd, had been set up to run the family business, which was no longer groceries, but Naseem himself. What Brendan had predicted years ago was really happening. Naseem was making millions and the wild figure that Brendan had suggested – £40 million – looked like being an underestimate. For Naseem's family, it had taken a little time for the reality of wealth to sink in. Riath and Nabeel were still buying lottery tickets. When an acquaintance saw them he said, 'What are you doing that for? You've already won the lottery, with Naz.'

From the outside, it appeared that the Brendan–Naseem partnership had survived a difficult period during which mutual respect had broken down. Naseem, like most adolescents, had naturally denied the father figure in order to mark out his own ground. He had been through the healthy, obnoxious stage, and had emerged.

Much of the pain had been caused because each exaggerated his own contribution to the partnership and diminished the other's. Naseem's sole attribution of his powers to God implied that Brendan's teaching was merely incidental to his success. Equally, Brendan's contention that almost anyone taught the system from day one could go all the way – after all, even Johnny Nelson had reached world level – was a denial of what Brendan himself knew and had known since the first day he saw him fighting – that Naseem had an exceptional gift.

Nevertheless, the tension seemed to have subsided, as if they both recognised that they needed each other. There was another startling realisation: while he had neglected training, and largely ignored Brendan's advice, Naseem had won twelve fights, secured a world title and defended it four times. Pulling together, there was no telling what Naseem and Brendan might achieve.

Brendan made his way to the car park at the side of the hotel while Naseem's Porsche roared away from the front entrance. It had been raining and the tarmac was dry where the car had been parked. On the tarmac, a sign in white paint was revealed: disabled.

There was rather more to Naseem's renewed dedication to hard work than reconciliation with Brendan or fear that the Medina episode might be repeated, or even respect for Johnson's credentials. Precedents and warnings were crowding in and had insinuated a tiny crack in the edifice of Naseem's self-belief, his assumption of invincibility. Naseem had been as amazed as everyone else in boxing by two devastating upsets in the closing months of 1996. First, Mike Tyson, the so-called baddest man on the planet, had been beaten, indeed beaten up, by Evander Holyfield. 'We watched it together,' said Frank Warren. 'Naseem was really shocked. It was obvious that Tyson hadn't trained as he should have done. He didn't take it seriously because he believed he could do it all on power. That was when Naseem realised the same could happen to him.'

Naseem was given a more directly relevant example of how the script can change when the Mexican super-bantamweight, Marco Antonio Barrera, was beaten. Hitherto, the careers of Barrera and Naseem had run in parallel. They were born within a month of one another. They were both prodigies, both knockout artists, both unbeaten, and both had huge followings. Barrera's record was even better than Naseem's. He had turned professional at fifteen and had won all his forty-one fights. Naseem had moved up to the featherweight division, but that would be no real obstacle to a showdown.

Naseem against Barrera promised to be by far the most lucrative fight ever among the lighter weights.

To encourage the clamour, Naseem attended Barrera's title defence against an American challenger, Junior Jones, in Miami on 22 November 1996. Victory for Barrera was assumed and Naseem's purpose was to make himself visible at ringside before and during the fight and to issue challenges once Jones was reclining on the canvas. Instead, he watched open-mouthed as Barrera was first hurt and then knocked cold by Jones.

'You can't take anything for granted in this game, and remember that what God gives, God can take away,' said Frank Warren. 'Watch out against Johnson. This guy is a quality fighter. Don't underestimate him.'

When Johnson arrived in London, he was informed that Naseem had labelled the contest Britain and the Arab world against the United States. 'This is not country against country,' Johnson said. 'It is not a war. Have we all gotten to such a state that when we face each other we have to say it's about countries? This is a sport between two men and at the end of the day life goes on. I have won six title fights in Europe and I didn't do it for the United States. I did it for Tom Johnson.'

For once, Naseem had met his match in the mind-game. When the protagonists met two days before the fight at a press conference at the London Arena, Naseem tried the gambit that had proved so effective against Steve Robinson: 'Let's make it winner take all, put both purses in a pot.'

But Johnson was not to be cowed. 'We can do that but I tell you – we go to these rules. We'll alleviate [*sic*] the officials. We'll take off the gloves and fight till death us do part.'

'You would then be in even worse trouble – knocked out in the first round,' said Naseem. 'You might not even get home. It ain't going to be a long trip – you'll be in the graveyard.'

Some of those present remembered a similar press conference two years earlier, when Gerald McClellan, who was soon to fight Nigel Benn, said: 'You have to go to war and in war you have to be prepared to die. That's what boxing is.' Four days later, McClellan was taken from the ring on a stretcher, with brain damage from which he would never recover.

In any case, as Johnson pointed out, 'You don't need to hype this fight.' The London Arena, which holds 12,500, with the most expensive ringside seats at £250, was sold out; Showtime would screen the fight live in America; Sky, for the first time, was going pay-per-view with a fight in Britain as the main event. Like the Tyson–Bruno fight, it was to be a huge commercial success.

For the first two rounds, and the first two minutes of the third round, the fight between Naseem and Tom Johnson resembled a formal dance from the age of manners, the two engaging and retreating, acknowledging each other with nods of respect. Johnson was very polished, slick and orthodox; Naseem less orthodox but equally refined. It was all very laudable, civilised and interesting.

Suddenly, all hell was let loose. When Naseem started it with a brutal attack with both hands, it somehow seemed reprehensible. He had spoilt the choreography, broken the aesthetic spell. But, after all, it was a fight as well as a boxing match, and Johnson was not surprised. He absorbed the first attack and launched a left to the head – missed – a right to the body – connected – and another left to the head – missed again as Naseem swayed, taking his head out of range while keeping his feet close, planted, ready to counter. Soon they were both punching, hands, arms, every nerve and instinct taut, never more alive, attacking and slipping out of trouble simultaneously. It was mayhem, but it had its own pattern and beauty, and, since it was on the very edge, it exhibited infinitely more skill than the opening eight minutes.

For the first time, an advantage had become apparent. More often than not, Naseem was hitting and Johnson missing. They broke off for a moment, and Naseem smiled. He dangled his hands by his side as Johnson gathered his breath. The first sign of contempt. Back in they went. Johnson fired a straight left and Naseem ducked. As he rose, he threw a right hand like a spear and caught Johnson to the chin. He was hurt. Naseem piled in, left and right, both grazing Johnson's face.

Johnson was weakened, his footwork, previously so precise, suddenly wobbled in disarray. This was the round – the third – in which Naseem and his mother had predicted Johnson would fall, and with seconds left of the round he looked ready to go. Naseem hurled another scything hook with the right, but Johnson was ready for it. He ducked and came up with a long-range punch that started somewhere near his boots and travelled in an arc like a tracer bullet. Naseem was watching it, and moving away, twisting from it, but it followed him, and when Naseem could bend no more, it found him. It wasn't full power, for it was at the end of its journey, almost spent. Otherwise, it might have knocked Naseem out. As it was, it knocked him downwards. Already leaning back, he lost his balance like a failing limbo dancer and touched down on the canvas with his right glove. As he did so, the bell rang.

The best-laid plans and intentions of almost every opponent of Naseem are jettisoned as soon as they have felt his power. Almost invariably, their boxing becomes fearful, unbalanced and over-cautious. But although Johnson had felt the full force of Naseem's punches, and had momentarily lost the coordination of his legs, he had not panicked as others had before him.

Still moving well, bobbing his head and looking for openings, Johnson survived the fourth and fifth rounds without serious mishap. His task was made easier by Naseem, who was hardly throwing a punch other than a hook, attempting to knock out Johnson rather than score or wear him out. In the centre of the front row at ringside, Frank Warren, never the most relaxed spectator, was shouting 'Bring them up! Bring them up!' He wanted to see uppercuts and short digs to the ribs, the shots that could hardly miss from short range. But Naseem persisted and Johnson evaded the heavy hooks with increasing ease. All three judges marked down the sixth round as Johnson's. Sharp and well organised, he had caught Naseem twice more with his right hand and had established some control.

As Johnson continued to impress in the opening stages of the seventh round, the arguments in his favour were stacking up. He had not been intimidated before the fight; he had survived the onslaught in the third round; he was experienced over a long fight and his tight defence and straight punching must be impressing the judges. But one convincing argument can defeat a hundred minor points. Naseem, who was beginning to look concerned and frustrated, at last succeeded in landing a left hook and immediately Johnson was again in deep trouble, his legs feeble, his hands wholly defensive, covering up.

This time the bell was Johnson's friend, but a minute's grace and a few words of advice were never going to be sufficient. Naseem could hardly wait for the eighth to begin. He was looking for the kill and connecting as he pleased, driving Johnson around the ring as easily as a child mistreating a doll. Johnson survived for two minutes. He retreated to the ropes, wounded. Naseem backed off for a second. He needed space. He turned his left shoulder and gave a twitch of his left hand. It was the dummy and Johnson bought it: he was no longer in the business of distinguishing between pretend punches and real ones. Every movement Naseem made threatened him. Indeed, Naseem had not dummied or withheld a punch in the round thus far. To do so now was genius. Johnson obliged and dipped to his left to avoid a left hook. As he did so, Naseem turned his body to the right and brought up the uppercut, invisible and deadly, meeting Johnson as he moved the other way. The bullfighter should kill with a single thrust, and Naseem, knowing that he had hit Johnson with a punch that must be decisive, stepped away to view his crumpling downfall.

At ringside, Naseem was presented with a birthday cake, three days early, in the form of two red gloves decorated with the word SKY. 'Thanks to Sky Sports,' said Naseem. 'Thanks to Frank Warren, the best promoter in the world. Respect to the sponsor, Adidas. Thanks especially to my father, I love him dearly, and my mum who basically said I was going to win in style. I just thank God for my abilities, my strength, for finishing the fights the way I finish. It all comes from Allah. I know I'm blessed with a gift from God and you can't beat a gift.'

A little later, Naseem visited Johnson in his dressing room. 'You the young gun,' said the fallen champion, who had made a remarkable recovery. Naseem admitted to Johnson that for a couple of years he hadn't run or really trained, but that for this fight he had made an exception.

'You must take it serious,' said Johnson. 'Don't go back to the bad habits. You must respect the title as I did. If you take it lightly there will be other young guns who will come along and defeat you.'

Frank Warren was ecstatic. He had been worried during the fifth and sixth rounds for he hated to see Naseem caught when it wasn't necessary. But he understood that Naseem had the devil in him, that he could not resist getting into a trial of strength, that he lived for the pleasure of close combat. Naseem had justified all Warren's claims to the Americans. Don King, who had taken Johnson to win, and who had lost an enormous bet, pronounced himself convinced. Warren's fighter was indeed something special. Showtime executives hailed Naseem as the next great star, who must now be properly introduced to the American public by fighting in the States.

Warren's birthday present for Naseem, who was about to be twenty-three, was rather more welcome than Sky's cake. It was an Aston Martin Vantage, a special edition that featured among its accessories a voice-activated video camera enabling the driver to watch what was happening behind the car on a screen on the dashboard. NAS 1, which had an engraved metal plate on the sill by the passenger door, reading BUILT BY ASTON MARTIN LAGONDA ESPECIALLY FOR PRINCE NASEEM HAMED, cost £200,000.

The Johnson fight was also vindication for Brendan. But even as the cheers rang around the London Arena, he felt strangely flat. The night Naseem had beaten Robinson had been an anticlimax as well. Brendan had dreamed and worked for years to train a world champion and when it happened it somehow lost its meaning.

Johnson had been beaten, the world title unified, the doubters silenced, the Americans convinced, the system proven, but Brendan felt subdued. He didn't want to celebrate with the others. Instead of returning to the dressing room, he sat alone in a corner of the arena as the crowd dispersed. He was thrilled with the way Naseem had finished the fight. The feint and the uppercut – shades once again of Dan Stewart and the third button on the waistcoat – was as good a move and as well executed as any they had rehearsed. But for Brendan, Naseem had not boxed well. He could have beaten Johnson much more easily if he had moved and slipped, boxed and not relied on power. He could have done to Johnson what he did to Belcastro. Naseem had made a hard job of what should have been much easier. He had put so much effort into his punches that he was tense, missing the target. His timing was off. He had kept trying to catch Johnson with the rocket-launcher. That had made him open to the counter, especially, yet again, to the right.

There had also been trouble before the fight, not for the first time, with Naseem's entourage. They had all stayed in the Grosvenor House Hotel, where Naseem had a suite, and two of them, Thomas Bradley, a sparring partner and sidekick of Naseem's, and Ali, Naseem's brother, had almost come to blows. Thomas Bradley was a dead ringer for Robbie Fowler, the Liverpool footballer, and he was usually as chirpy. But he had a bad temper. Ali Hamed had a short fuse, too. Although he had been as talented a boxer as Naseem, he had never had sufficient discipline to succeed. At the root of the bad blood between them was rivalry for Naseem's attention. It started to get extremely tense and it looked like a fight might break out in the room, which would certainly have been wrecked. Brendan was tempted to let them get on with it, but any sort of trouble at this stage could have dire consequences, and he had to intervene.

'Just shut it, you two. We don't need upset now. The only thing that matters is Naz winning. Then you can bash each other up.'

In the early days, there had been no entourage. It had been Brendan, Naseem and John. Now it was the brothers, whose presence Brendan resented, as well as assorted friends and hangers-on. The tension and competition removed a lot of the happiness for Brendan. Instead of savouring the moment, he wondered whether the time had come to walk away. Naseem had trained well and he had beaten Johnson but he still hadn't listened. Why not quit while they were in front? Why hang around and watch Naseem destroy himself? Why be around on the night he was going to get beaten?

# Nabeel Hamed's Story

*I was born in 1970, a year after my older brother, Riath, and four years before my younger brother, Naseem. There were nine children in our family, five boys and four girls. The younger ones got looked after more than me and Riath. We had our fights like all families, but we always stuck together and we still do. My dad was a real man, a survivor. He stuck there through the hard times, working in the steelworks before buying the shop. We were taught right and wrong, not to steal or hurt anybody. It was a strict Muslim family and we were brought up in the Arab tradition. We spoke Arabic in the house and English outside.*

*In the shop, we all took it in turns to serve, except Naz who got away with it by always going down to the gym. We all went through the same schools. There were hardly any Asians or Arabs and because we were different we were abused. It wasn't physical so much, and our dad had said never be afraid of anything, so we knew that if fighting comes, you have to take it. But we were called Paki and Black Bastard and the shop windows were smashed by the National Front. Our dad wanted us to feel secure and learn how to fight, and he decided to take us to the gym down the road. We met Brendan Ingle. He was a really nice guy and he said 'No problem, Sal, I'll take care of your sons', and he asked dad for £5 for each of us to join the club.*

*At first, me and Riath didn't want Naseem to come with us to the gym. He was only seven and so skinny you would have laughed at him if you'd seen him in those days. We thought he was going to get hurt so we said he couldn't come with us. He started crying and we felt sorry for him so we said we'll all go down together. On the first day, Brendan said we should just watch the boxing. Naz loved it. He was dying to get in the ring. The next day we started on the footwork. That lasted about two weeks. Then Brendan said we could spar. We didn't have any gloves but Alma passed some to Naz and he went in first. Everything he had learned in the first two weeks, he did in the ring. He could hit this guy where he wanted and the guy couldn't hit him back. Brendan always taught defence first. He's a genius at teaching people not to get hit.*

*Riath drifted out after about a year and I stayed for eight years. I had seventeen amateur fights and lost four, but I was working as a mechanic and didn't have time to go to the gym every day. It's all about dedication. Me and Riath didn't have it and Naz did.*

*Herol Graham and Brian Anderson were the main men in the gym and they had wicked music. Naz really wanted one of their tapes. So one day when they were in the shower I took it and raced home and copied it and then slipped it back without them knowing. Herol was like Steve Davis, the snooker player. In those days, they were both unbeatable. But in the end Herol thought all he had to do was turn up. Also, he didn't have a big heart like Naz.*

*I used to spar with Naz quite a lot. He hurt me with his body shots. He's got a chopping sort of shot that really gets you to the side. I watched Naz box whenever I could and saw nearly every fight he had as an amateur. Brendan's mentality was that you don't need family around when you're fighting and there was a little bit of conflict about that even in those days. Naz loved it when I was there to watch him and Brendan didn't realise that we stick together as a family.*

*I believe Naz has a gift from God because nobody could be that good. Nothing can hurt his concentration. He changes in the ring. He becomes a monster, like an assassin. Naz thinks differently from other fighters. He's a winner. He's a very wise guy. He's had a good trainer and mentor in Brendan but he's learned from his father and brothers as well. I don't think Naz and Brendan will ever split up, but there have been plenty of problems. Naz needed to think for himself, to grow up, but he still loves Brendan. The trouble with Brendan is that he doesn't let you answer. He asks a question and answers it himself. He teaches you life skills and he can talk about anything without embarrassment, but he would want you to sign a contract when you're seven years old.*

*After working as a mechanic, I worked at Texas Homecare as a sales adviser for five years. Then I set up Naz's fan club, as a hobby at first. It was my idea. Naz used to keep every letter he got and reply to them. When he was on ITV, he got floods of letters. Some people loved him and some hated him, but they were always interested. They're not boxing fans, they're the new generation. They love Naz as a pure winner. He's changed British youth because he's got a super-confident attitude. People write in and say that thanks to Naz they have the confidence to stand up to bullies. We've got just under 10,000 members.*

*None of us in the family had any idea what was going to happen with Naz. I was more interested in his boxing than the others, and I knew he was good, but nobody can see the future, only God. His achievements still amaze us and we can't believe how big he's got. We just thank God for what's happened to our family. God has given Naz to our parents for all their hard work and it's changed all our lives.*

*Naz walks through fear. He prepares himself mentally for every fight. He's very generous to the family and he puts a smile on all our faces. We love him dearly. Only three years ago, we were living above the shop and now we've got big houses and nice cars and we thank God for everything. I've got a brand new BMW and Riath's got a Jaguar and a Shogun. Naz bought our dad a Mercedes and a car for our mum even though she can't drive, plus all the sisters. People say we're riding on his back but it's not true. Me and Riath work hard for what we've got. We make Naz a lot of money and we make the family a lot of money and we love it.*

*Naz's money is getting looked after good style by Riath. Me and Riath want to build an empire. We want to secure Naz's future for life. We want to keep the lifestyle we have now and all the family are working in his business. We're concentrating beyond boxing. We're expanding into property and show business. I can see Naz doing a movie. A lot of people laugh when they hear we're building an empire but it's better for us if they do. Wait and see.*

# CHAPTER NINETEEN
## Payback Time

The best approach for any boxer unfortunate enough to have to share a ring with Naseem might well have been to use the press conferences before the fight to soften him and cause confusion: 'I know I have no chance, but it's a great privilege, a dream come true, to box the Prince, who is peerless and magnificent. I just hope I can do myself justice and remember something to tell my grandchildren after I have been beaten.'

The worst mistake, of course, was to belittle him. After Tom Johnson, Naseem's next opponent was Billy Hardy, a tough veteran from Sunderland. Hardy had twice fought and lost a world title challenge. He was the European and Commonwealth champion and had beaten Steve Robinson to become the mandatory challenger for Naseem's WBO world title. But as a fighter he didn't belong in the same list, let along the same ring.

Hardy might have survived long enough to have an argument if Naseem had taken him lightly, or if the divisions between Brendan and Naseem had begun to have a more serious effect on Naseem's performance. But any chance Hardy had of achieving the most limited objective disappeared at the press conference called to announce the fight.

Mistake number one was to call Naseem a kid. The last opponent to make a similar remark had been another veteran, Freddy Cruz, who called Naseem a child and was tortured for it.

Mistake number two was for Hardy to bring along his trainer, Gordon Ibinson, the man who as an amateur referee had given Naseem a standing count for holding his hands too low. Ibinson was also one of the amateur officials Brendan believed had been instrumental in getting him banned.

Mistake number three was for Hardy to reveal he would be training in Sheffield with Glyn Rhodes, a former boxer of Brendan's who had set up a rival gym across the city, and Herol Graham, who would give advice on Naseem's style and moves.

This was all too much for Brendan, who publicly branded Glyn Rhodes (no relation of Ryan Rhodes) and Herol Graham 'snakes'. As for Naseem, what he might have seen solely as an easy payday became 'payback time'. Whenever he felt bored with training over the following few weeks, Naseem said to Brendan: 'Keep telling me what they did to you those years ago. I'm going to make sure we get our own back.'

For several weeks before Hardy unwittingly united Brendan, Naseem and everyone associated with the St Thomas's club, the rift between Brendan and Naseem had been growing more obvious. Indeed, the gym could be divided into three camps: pro-Brendan, pro-Naseem, and torn between the two. 'I've got the best team in the gym ever,' Brendan said, 'apart from two.' He would then invite a member of the gym to identify the two odd ones out. Everyone knew they were Naseem and his youngest brother, Ali, and said so. Even Naseem's best friends in the gym, Johnny Nelson and Ryan Rhodes, reluctantly admitted as much.

'We thought we'd created the ultimate fighter, but he's flawed,' Brendan said in despair. 'How can you spend sixteen years explaining the seven deadly sins – envy, jealousy, greed, sloth, anger, lust and gluttony – and then he falls straight into the trap?' Brendan's version of the seven deadly sins was imperfect. Pride, envy, sloth, gluttony, covetousness, anger and lust made up the usual list, but even if Naseem had signed up for a few, even a majority, it was a strange idea that a fighter needed to be a saint.

Two weeks before the Hardy fight, a Sky TV crew filmed an interview with Brendan that was to be used as part of the build-up. The interview was conducted by Adam Smith, whose passive manner was in sharp contrast to most Sky presenters, but who was intelligently effective at persuading his subjects to open up. Brendan sat on a wooden chair in the centre of the gym, and allowed himself to be beguiled into dropping hints that all was not well between himself and Naseem.

'Can anyone beat Naz?'

'He can beat himself. If you start thinking you're chocolate, you might start eating yourself.'

'Is he doing that already?'

'In the Medina fight, he did, yes.'

'Is he training hard? Is he running?'

'He says he's running, but he's not training as hard as he did for the Johnson fight. Mind you, for that fight he over-trained.'

'What about Hardy?'

'The worst thing Hardy did was call him a kid.'

'Glyn Rhodes and Herol Graham training Hardy – does that upset you?'

'Herol Graham couldn't train white mice. To train, you need the patience of Job.'

'In five years' time, will you still be part of the Naz story?'

'We have differences of opinion. He can be very difficult to deal with. Sometimes I've had to bite my lip and walk away. Other times, he's as good as gold. But he's been no different since he was seven. I know that when boxers get beaten, the first thing that happens is that the trainer gets the sack. But I won't be upset. Naz wants to be the gaffer in here. But I'm the gaffer in here and they can like it or lump it. When I'm dead, they'll think, that old bastard taught us something, maybe we should have listened.'

Those beating a path to the gym had grown ever more cosmopolitan. A Japanese sports writer spent several days preparing a feature article for a magazine. His conclusion couldn't have pleased Brendan more: 'You have many Naseems.' A fax came from the private office of His Royal Highness Prince Khaled Bin Sultan Abdulaziz of Saudi Arabia: 'Prince Khaled's sons, Fahad and Abdullah are fanatical supporters of Prince Naseem. Would like to come to watch training. Friday would suit best.' On Friday they came, in a Rolls-Royce, young lads, real princes.

Early one evening, when the gym was in full swing, thirty boxers training, Naseem arrived. On his way to the gym in the Porsche he had stopped off for a hamburger and chips because he felt hungry. It didn't affect his sparring. He went in with Johnny Nelson and was as brilliant as usual. But the big stir during the session was not Naseem but Daniel Teasdale, a precocious fourteen-year-old who was to Naseem what Naseem had once been to Herol Graham: the next star.

Teasdale was already a schoolboy champion, and more skilful than Naseem had been at the same age. Just as the young Naseem had been taken everywhere by Brendan, so Teasdale's education included attending boxing shows, sitting in dressing rooms and sparring with professionals, some of whom, already, couldn't touch him. He had just returned from a trip more glamorous than any young Naseem had enjoyed. His airline ticket paid for by a combination of his father, the club and Ryan Rhodes, Teasdale had been out to Las Vegas, chaperoned by two journalists, Claude Abrams of *Boxing News* and Steve Bunce of the *Daily Telegraph*, who were covering one of the year's big fights, Oscar De La Hoya against Pernell Whitaker. It was Teasdale's first time in the gym since his return and he couldn't contain his excitement, running around with stories of grand hotels, meetings with stars, and the great fight itself, which was won by De La Hoya (though Teasdale scored it for Whitaker), as well as his own tale, of how he had had no ticket but had managed to slip past the guards and ended up watching from the $500 seats.

Teasdale had brought back presents: fight programmes and T-shirts for Brendan and Ryan Rhodes.

'Where's mine, then?' said Naseem.

'I didn't get you one.'

'Why not?'

'You didn't help me to get over there.'

Naseem wandered off, his displeasure obvious.

Teasdale could almost match the young Naseem for front. An expert on American attitudes after one visit, he declared: 'Naz is too arrogant. They won't like that in America. They won't like that look of his. You can be flash without being arrogant.'

Naseem went back into the ring, going several more rounds on the pads, which were held by Dominic, Brendan's youngest son. Dominic had only recently become involved in helping Brendan and John Ingle to train Naseem, but his was a good influence. He worked Naseem hard. Dominic, who worked out regularly with weights, was fourteen stone and solid. To be effective, the man holding the pads has to be trainer and opponent, calling the shots to be thrown but also pushing the boxer about, resisting him physically, messing him around, moving in and out of range. For the boxer, a round on the pads should be harder than a round of sparring, with no respite. But for the man holding the pads, it can be dangerous. Brendan used to dread an accident when John, who was relatively light, was holding the pads and Naseem was hitting full out. He knew only too well what could happen. Brendan's eldest brother, Jimmy, the one who before the war had been European amateur champion, settled in Luton and used to help train lads at the Luton Irish Club. In his mid-sixties, he was holding the pads and was hit on the chin. He never properly recovered and was dead a few weeks later.

Another virtue of using Dominic was that mentally he was tougher than Brendan or John. He wouldn't stand for any nonsense, and Naseem knew it. Dominic took after Alma, while John took after Brendan. If Brendan was collecting the subs for the gym, a sob story would probably work. If John was collecting them, it might be worth trying for a postponement. If Dominic was collecting, you paid up.

With a week to go before the fight, Dominic's work on the pads and Hardy's presence in Sheffield were having their full effect. Naseem was below nine stone, which proved that he could easily make the super-bantamweight limit again if required.

Relations with Brendan had improved. One evening, when Brendan went into the hotel steam room to give Naseem a massage, he found Naseem had for once arrived first and at the arranged time. As he pushed open the door, Brendan could make out Naseem as well as two men and a girl in the corner. Brendan laid down the towels and reached for his bottle of oil. 'Hope you don't mind,' he said. 'I'm going to give him a rub.' The four of them burst out laughing because

Naseem had predicted exactly what Brendan would say when he came in and had mimicked him perfectly.

Soon there was another sign of affection. A few days before the fight, Brendan was unwell. After training, Naseem asked, 'Are you going to give me a rub?' Brendan said he wasn't feeling too good. Naseem looked concerned and said, 'Don't bother with the rub. You go to bed. I'll have a steam by myself and then go home.'

Using Dominic was in part an admission by Brendan, who suffered mildly from arthritis, that when he took Naseem on the pads himself, he found it painful to absorb the punches, even through thick padding. But during one of Naseem's final training sessions for Hardy, Brendan took him for a couple of rounds and Naseem murdered the pads. When he finished, he thanked Brendan and told him quietly he was going to hurt Hardy, break his nose and beat him up.

At the final press conference, on 28 April 1997, Hardy's camp compounded their folly. Gordon Ibinson admitted he had penalised Naseem in an amateur contest. 'It was in Liverpool,' he said. 'I gave him a standing count for dropping his hands. In amateur boxing that amounts to a knockdown because he wasn't defending himself.'

Hardy tried to sound convincing. 'At the moment, it's Prince Naz. On Saturday night, it will be King William. In one breath Naz is saying this is the hardest he's ever trained, and in the next he says he's going to knock me out in one round and doesn't need to train. How do you work it out?'

Sometimes, as Hardy was to soon discover, the truth is indeed contradictory.

On the day of the fight, Naseem was as relaxed as ever. His only concern was that the early pay-per-view sales, of which he was to receive a proportion, were very low. They would remain low. Naseem spent much of the day, and the previous evening, in the company of a young boy suffering from leukaemia. He had met the boy on a recent hospital visit and had invited him to the fight. They watched videos in Naseem's hotel suite and rode around Manchester with Naseem at the wheel of a hired Lamborghini. On the afternoon of the fight Naseem played snooker, and with only three hours to wait, he left his hotel and went to the Nynex Arena to watch a friend and gym-mate, Anas Oweida, who was fighting on the undercard. Having congratulated his friend on victory, Naseem returned to the hotel to rest before setting off again to fight Hardy.

The fight was brutal and short. It lasted ninety-three seconds. Naseem's first full punch broke Hardy's nose and put him down for a count of seven. A left hook put him down again for a count of six, after which the referee called a halt.

Afterwards, while he was being interviewed on the ring apron, Naseem put his arm round Brendan. To all outward appearances, it was just like old times.

## Daniel Teasdale's Story

*I started coming to the gym when I was six. That's nine years ago now. It were me dad who brought me, because he thought it would help bring me out of myself, which it did, eventually. I had a lot of problems at home, because me mum and dad split up and I had to deal with it on me own. I haven't got any brothers or sisters. We lived on a farm outside Sheffield. I lived with me mum in a caravan at the back of the farm and me dad lived in the house with Grandad and Granny, where he grew up. Nobody would sit down and talk to me and I were always on me own. I wouldn't talk to anybody, and I had to have these psychiatrists to help me out.*

*Dad is a taxidermist. He was really getting on in his career in them days and he was always in the workshop. He hated coming in because me mum was always shouting at him. She is from Sri Lanka. She didn't have anything to do with her time. She never occupied herself. Then, to top it all, she turned Jehovah's Witness. She dragged me to these meetings and put me with these people, Jehovah's Witnesses, who talked to me, overpowered me, and I couldn't deal with it. That's why I didn't want to talk to anybody or associate with anybody. Then I went to live with me dad.*

*I didn't want to box at all, at first. I hated boxing. I went on Saturday mornings and a lot of the other kids thought I was daft or something because I wouldn't talk to anybody. There was a certain kid who used to beat me up.*

One day he smashed me front teeth in, in the gym. It was supposed to be just sparring to the body, but he hit me in the face, accidentally on purpose, like Brendan says.

That made me hate boxing even more, and on Friday nights I were so nervous I used to sleep with me dad, because when I slept on me own I used to think there were shadows on the walls, and it scared me. I used to be laying in bed with me dad asleep and I were frozen, not moving, because I thought if I move, me dad's going to wake up. But if I stay frozen and he doesn't wake up, we're going to be late for boxing and he'll say we might as well miss it this week. If he moved, I'd think, oh no, don't wake up, don't wake up, but he always did. He used to say to me at night, over and over, no fear, no fear, because I used to be afraid of me own shadow. Gradually, I understood that if I could get over it, I could live a normal life.

The main thing that brought me out was when Brendan got me to go in the ring and sing. He told me it would exercise me vocal cords and give me confidence. At first there was no way anybody was going to get me in the ring to sing a song, because I wouldn't even talk to anybody. I saw everybody else doing it and I thought I wish I could do that, but then I'd say to meself I can't. When I did it, I sang

Red and yellow and pink and green,
Orange and purple and blue,
I can sing a rainbow, I can sing a rainbow.

Training was mainly footwork to begin with, going up and down the lines and getting everything off to perfection. Gradually I enjoyed it and I thought, I'm good at something, why don't I try to get better at it, and try to be the best I can be. I just practised and practised and listened. I always listened. There was this ginger-haired kid called Paul Barnes. I used to see him going up and down the lines and he were brilliant. I used to think, I'll never be as good as that. I saw him sparring and I thought if I could only be half as good as him, I'd appreciate it. So I got to know him and everything he did I wanted to do better. After a few months, we were good friends and I thought, this is it, I know I'm as good as him, I want to become better than him, and I worked and worked at it and got the lines off to perfection. I even made me own moves up.

Brendan taught me the basics and I made the movements even better. I can do movements what nobody knows, and I'm still improving them all the time.

When I was eleven or twelve I had my first amateur fight, in Leeds. I thought it would be a lot tougher than it was. I thought it would be like one of those *Rocky IV* fights, a real punch-up, but it was nothing like that. First round, I was so used to body-sparring in the gym, I was just hitting him to the body, and when I went back to the corner, John Ingle said what are you doing? you're supposed to be hitting him to the head, you're not playing around in the gym now, you're not playing marbles, it's time to do what you've come here to do. So I went out in the second and third rounds and put everything into it, hitting him to the head and body, and I won.

Then I had trouble with me mum again. She knew I was getting on in boxing but she said: No Daniel, you don't want to be fighting, Daniel. God wouldn't like it. You don't want to go in to hurt other people and you don't want to get hurt yourself. That used to scare me. I thought, what if I hurt him, what if I damage him, what if I kill him? I didn't want to kill anybody. But then me dad said, look he goes in there knowing that if he dies in there, he's died doing something he wants to do.

Last year, Brendan got me going to gymnastics classes. He wanted me to be more flexible, but also so that I can do all the flips and somersaults, like Naz and Ryan Rhodes. But I can do more than them because they never went to gymnastics. Then Brendan said that now that I can do the gymnastics pretty well, I should start off on tap-dancing, because if I can do gymnastics and tap-dance it'll help my movement and it'll bring in a lot of publicity, so I've started tap-dancing lessons.

I've got me confidence now and in my mind there's nobody in the world at my age and weight who can beat me. In the national schoolboy finals last year I stopped my opponent in twenty-one seconds. He was nervous, I think. I had these really nice shorts and a red top and I was dazzling. Everybody was cheering and I thought I'd better put on a good performance. I threw everything at him and the referee stopped the fight. I thought, that's brilliant, I'm beating Naz's records now. Naz didn't like it because he wants to be the best in the gym, and if anyone's going to be better than him, he's not going to like it. He's a brilliant fighter and I admire him for what he's done and the *way he boxes, but he doesn't appreciate what Brendan's done for him. He thinks he's done it all on his own.*

# CHAPTER TWENTY
## Money Has Become Your God

The circumstances leading to Naseem's fight against Juan Cabrera, which followed the slaughter of Billy Hardy, brought Brendan and Naseem to the brink of divorce. In most respects, the Cabrera fight, in July 1997 at Wembley, was unremarkable: another foregone conclusion, another notch on the belt. But in Naseem's personal development, and in his relationship with Brendan, it was a major milestone on a downhill journey.

If 1995 had been the year of breakthrough for Naseem and 1996 the year of warnings, he seemed determined to make 1997 the year of indulgence and extravagance. It was not an unnatural desire. Any young man in his early twenties who finds himself worshipped and wealthy has to be forgiven for tasting the fruit, and Naseem had dedicated himself to boxing from the age of seven. He was due some fun.

At the turn of 1997, Naseem bought his parents a house costing £300,000 in the leafy part of Sheffield. He provided a wardrobe of new clothes for his mother, Caira, and a Mercedes 500SL saloon for his father. In May, he apparently went further. Newspapers reported that Naseem turned up at his parents' house with two black plastic bin liners. With Sal and Caira watching in astonishment, Naseem was said to have turned the bags upside down and tipped the contents on to the living-room carpet: £500,000 in bundles of £50 notes. 'That's your spending money for the next six months,' he was reported to have said.

When Brendan read the story, he didn't know whether to believe it or not. But he reckoned he knew its genesis. Years before, as Naseem well knew because Brendan had told him, there had been a similar incident at Brendan's house. It happened in 1975. Brendan had retired from boxing and was unemployed. He decided to make a comeback. In a story that appeared in the *Star*, Brendan was quoted as saying 'I'm up before five every morning doing my roadwork and sparring at night. I plan to have a good crack at a comeback because I could do with a few extra quid, but I'll have to cut back if I get a job.'

The day the article appeared, Brendan arrived home at tea-time to find his children in tears. They had been teased at school. 'Now everyone knows we're skint,' they wailed. The next day, Brendan went to see a friend who was a scrap-metal dealer, and borrowed £500 in £1 notes. When the children came back from school, Brendan took them into the sitting room and threw the bundle of notes into the air. 'Pick that lot up,' he said. 'And don't let anyone tell you that we're skint.'

A few weeks after his own demonstration of wealth, Naseem split up with his girlfriend, Eleasha Elphinstone, who, despite her exotic name, was a down-to-earth Yorkshire girl, a hairdresser from Wakefield. She was beautiful and blonde, but not dumb. They had met in a club in Sheffield. Naseem very rarely mentioned her in public and in interviews, even when pressed by writers of feature articles, always refused to discuss the relationship. She had been most visible at ringside, sitting in the favoured seat next to Frank Warren in the centre of the front row for the fights against Johnson and Hardy. After the Johnson fight, Naseem had announced he was going to take a few weeks off, 'chilling out with Eleasha', and they went on holiday to California. There were two versions of their first break-up: that she walked out when Naseem refused to let her go with him to a nightclub in Sheffield; and that he dumped her after she refused to convert to Islam.

Soon after splitting up with Eleasha, and only a few weeks after his driving licence had been returned following a year's ban for speeding in the Porsche, Naseem went off to a nightclub with a group of friends and was involved in two car crashes. Driving a Ferrari Berlinetta F355, which he had taken out on trial (the Aston Martin was in for repairs after being scratched), Naseem lost control at a roundabout leading to the M18 at Doncaster and smashed into a crash barrier. It was just after two o'clock in the morning. With the driver's door wedged solid,

Naseem had to climb out by the passenger door but was unhurt. He later said he had swerved to avoid a fox. The Ferrari was a write-off.

The drama continued. Four of Naseem's friends were following some distance behind the Ferrari, in a Vauxhall Nova. When Naseem had extricated himself from the Ferrari, he flagged them down and climbed into the back. They were about to move off when they were hit from behind by a van. The Vauxhall, too, was wrecked.

Naseem's training was equally manic and erratic. Although he was to fight Juan Cabrera, his original opponent was another Argentinian, Pastor Maurin. Naseem had seen a video of Maurin, an unbeaten but moderate fighter, and had decided he would knock him out in two rounds. He also concluded he wouldn't need to train overmuch. On the last day of June, with a little over two weeks before he was due to meet Maurin, Naseem turned up at the gym, a notable event in itself, and put in a hard and extraordinary session that had about it a hint of recklessness and self-destruction. At one point, sparring with Johnny Nelson, Naseem threw himself forward, flying three or four feet through the air, across the ring and upwards, to land a right-hand lead. Even Nelson, who had clocked up countless rounds with Naseem in every mood, shook his head in disbelief. When he had finished sparring, Naseem threw himself out of the ring, diving feet first between the ropes to land on the gym floor three feet below. The slightest slip would have guaranteed injury.

Brendan's most frequent gesture during what was supposed to be the hardest period of training was shaking his head. He was worried that Naseem might pull out of the fight. He felt humiliated when he went across town to the hotel steam room to give Naseem a massage and had to wait an hour or more for him to arrive; sometimes he had to pack his gear and leave because Naseem hadn't bothered to turn up at all. He was sorry that Eleasha had departed, because he saw her as a stabilising influence and a counterbalance to what he thought was the undue control exerted over Naseem by his brothers. It irritated Brendan to learn of Naseem's generosity to his family when his own payment for the Hardy fight – formally from Naseem, but adminis-tered by his brother, Riath – had been made five weeks late.

Increasingly, Brendan believed that Naseem's family was an unhelpful influence, and that Riath was the worst of all.

But if it was true that Naseem abused Brendan, it was also true that Brendan allowed him to. What, for example, would Dominic have done if it had been his job to give Naseem a massage? He would have said, 'I'll meet you at eight, but don't be late.' And after five minutes with no Naseem, he would have gone. And if that had happened a couple of times, there would have been no more massages. Brendan always prided himself on being a student of human nature, and for years he had tried to instil into Naseem a certain morality, a code of conduct. But what Brendan failed to do was what Naseem needed most of all. He failed to say no.

It didn't help that Naseem knew he could beat almost any featherweight in the world without training. He could have come straight off holiday and beaten Hardy and Maurin on the same night, even if the pair of them had been preparing for months. But although a gifted boxer may win one or two fights without dedication, he won't last long, especially if he has to make a weight limit. If his weight fluctuates too much between contests, and he trains not to tune his timing and rehearse moves for the fight, but to remove weight, he will soon be in trouble.

Five days before the Wembley fight, Naseem was finishing a session on the heavy bag, sweat pouring from his upper body. Pastor Maurin had pulled out after his eye was cut in sparring and had been replaced by Juan Cabrera, the sparring partner who had done the damage. It made no difference to Naseem. Instead of Maurin being knocked out in two rounds, Cabrera would be knocked out in two rounds.

Naseem walked over to Brendan, who was talking to young Daniel Teasdale, and held out his right glove for Brendan to untie the lace. 'Take it off,' he ordered. Then he thrust the left glove towards Teasdale.

'Undo that.'

'Say please,' said Teasdale.

Naseem swung a punch that caught Teasdale in the stomach.

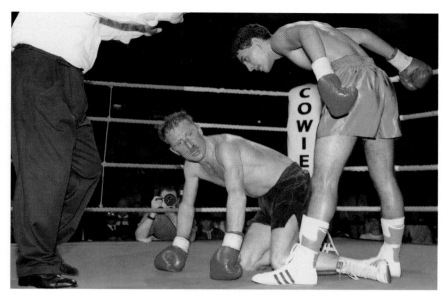

Tormentor: Naseem inquires about the health of a fallen
opponent, Des Gargano

Clown champion: Naseem in the last round of his European
title fight against Vincenzo Belcastro

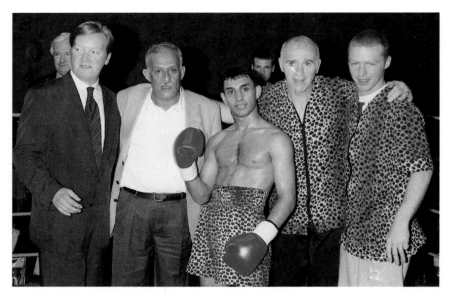

Aftermath: Naseem celebrates with Brendan and John Ingle,
his father Sal and Frank Warren

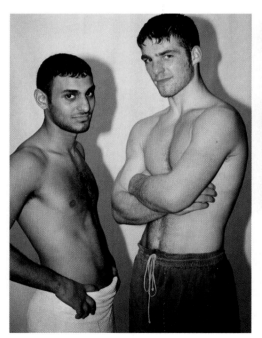

Holiday snaps: Brendan and
Naseem put on an exhibition
on the pads in the Yemen

Best mates and champions
both: Naseem and
Ryan Rhodes

Enter the dragon: Naseem pauses for a moment's reflection before his first world title fight, against Steve Robinson in Cardiff

Avenger: Billy Hardy made it personal, and paid the price

(*Facing page, above and below*) Unifier: Naseem, the WBO world feather-weight champion, defeats Tom Johnson the experienced IBF champion

The Full Monty: Naseem was faultless in beating Jose Badillo in Sheffield

Crunchtime in
the Big Apple:
Naseem's dramatic
encounter with
Kevin Kelley

Double Image: Naseem posing in front of himself,
New York, Christmas '97

Teasdale backed off, wounded. Turning to Brendan, he said: 'You ought to teach him some manners.'

From the following evening, Brendan kept a diary of events leading up to the fight.

### Tuesday July 15

Naz trained 5.30pm, trained with heavy gear on, finished around seven o'clock, went to Swallow Hotel to give him a rub-down, got in car, Naz drove like mad, up St Philips road, mobile phone rang, police followed and stopped Naz. The abuse Naz gave to the policeman was awful. If the fight hadn't been in three days [sic] I would have walked off. Naz was obnoxious. It is so sad. Money has become his God. He is kidding everyone. But worst of all he is kidding himself. All he wants to hear is please and praise, and having yes men around him. John picked me up at hotel. Went to London.

### Wednesday July 16

Press conference. Trained.

### Thursday July 17

Naz went to bed five o'clock in morning, got up late. Press conference. Weighed Naz after training. 9st 2½lbs.

### Friday July 18

Naz did not come in till around six o'clock in the morning. Got Naz up at twelve o'clock, noon. Weighed him. 9st 4½lbs. Got him to have a hot bath. Between twelve o'clock and four Naz had four hot baths and went to steam room. Got over 4lbs off him by half past five in the evening. He was 4ozs over. He put on sweat gear and shadow boxed for ten mins to get 4ozs off. He made the weight at the weigh-in. Went to eat and drink water at 6.30.

### Saturday July 19

Naz boxed brilliant. Cabrera stopped in the second round.

After the Cabrera fight, Brendan was in turmoil. It was shocking that Naseem had stayed out all night before the fight and that he had had to shed so much weight before the weigh-in. Naseem had behaved arrogantly. He had even hit Teasdale. Brendan had had to wait to be paid yet again, so that he felt 'like a beggar at the gate' and he was still sore that he wasn't getting the 25 per cent to which he believed he was entitled. He resented the fact that Riath, whose attitude and ability he questioned, was calling the shots.

But behind the rationalisation of those grievances, which Brendan confided to his family and a few close friends, there was something which he could not admit and which could not be resolved by negotiation or a better deal: rejection. Naseem had had to find himself, and in doing so had grown apart from Brendan. That was natural. And it was natural for Brendan to cling to the belief that Naseem would be destroyed if he didn't listen to Brendan and respect him. But there was a corollary: if Brendan discovered that in fact Naseem could do without him, he would be the one to be destroyed.

Brendan had already planned his course of action; had even rehearsed the conversation. His ten-fight contract with Naseem, which started with the first fight for Sky, had expired. Brendan travelled to Dublin for a three-day break and walked around his old haunts. It was there that he made up his mind. It was over. The next time he saw Naseem he would tell him and walk away for good.

Six weeks after the Cabrera fight, on 2 September, Frank Warren held a press conference in Sheffield to announce his plans for a huge promotion which he called The Full Monty, after the hit film which was also set in the city.

Naseem's behaviour at the press conference was pretty insufferable. Dozens of representatives of the press and television, as well as boxers and managers from all around the country, had assembled at the Sheffield Arena to learn about and disseminate news of an event that was of great importance to Frank Warren, Brendan and, apparently, Naseem. But Naseem, who had the shortest journey of all, arrived fifty minutes late, after driving the two miles across the city in a

Lamborghini Diablo, the fastest road car in the world. Having turned the mood of the occasion from expectation to irritation and boredom, Naseem insulted another world champion on the bill by telling him he was on 'my undercard', and declared that he didn't care who his opponent might be 'as long as that bank balance is getting fatter and fatter'. After the usual theatricals, Naseem refused to give an individual interview to any newspaper except the *Sun*, with whom he had recently signed an exclusive contract. Frank Warren, already irritated by Naseem's late arrival, was surprised and angry to learn of the deal with a paper he purported to loathe.

At the end of the press conference, Brendan took Naseem to one side for a private word.

'I don't want to train you any more.'

'What?'

'I don't want to train you any more. I'm sick of the last three years, and the last three fights have been worst of all. I don't want anything to do with you.'

Naseem looked around to see if anyone was within earshot. 'Not now. We'll talk later on.'

A crisis meeting was held that afternoon at Baldwin's Omega restaurant in the centre of Sheffield. Frank Warren and Naseem's brother, Riath, attended but first Brendan and Naseem spoke alone, sitting opposite each other at a table.

At last Brendan spelt out his grievances.

'I haven't been happy for the last three years, Naz, the way you've been training. The last three fights, it's been ridiculous. You've been cramming all your training into one session. I've got to the stage with all the hassle I've had, I don't want to train you any more, I don't want to be involved. The way you've been training, the way you've been behaving, you've been horrible.'

Naseem spoke gently. 'I know I haven't done everything right as I should have done. But I was fit for the Johnson fight.'

'No, for the Johnson fight you trained too hard. Really, Johnson shouldn't have got past two rounds with you. What you're doing now is terrible, you're going to beat yourself, and I don't want to be around when it happens.'

'Why didn't you tell me I wasn't training properly?'

'You wouldn't listen.'

Brendan produced the diary he had kept leading up to the Cabrera fight and passed it across for Naseem to read.

'I don't agree with that.'

'What?'

'That money's my God.'

'Why not?'

'There's only one God, Allah.'

'Naz, you shouldn't bring Allah into it.'

'I'm not. Religion is personal and private. That's what you always said. Religion is personal and private, politics is personal and private, and sex is personal and private.'

'Yes, they are. And you can't go on TV and say that God's helping you to knock them out.'

'Anyway, Brendan, money's your God.'

'What?'

'You've become greedy.'

'No, you've become greedy. You cut my money down from 25 per cent and then cut it down again.'

'But you've never managed me under Frank Warren. Frank's done everything. And you've been paid a lot of money. That's why you've got your gates and a new roof.'

'Frank's the brains of the outfit. But I've spent sixteen years on you. I have to train you and motivate you. Naz, listen, when you were doing it right I once kissed the floor in the gym and said you were as good as Muhammad Ali and you were going to be better. You were going to be the perfect fighter.'

'There's never been a perfect fighter.'

'You could have been the first one.'

'OK, from now on I'll train properly.'

'Really, Naz, if we're going to stay together, we've got to come to an understanding. You've got to do as you're told and you've got to train three times a day. Morning, evening and then run.'

'I'll do that.'

'The best thing to do, if we're going to stay together, is do this fight and see how we go on. If you're happy with me, fair enough. If I'm happy with you, fair enough. If not, then you sort yourself out. Also, we've got to agree what the money is.'

'All right, we'll do that.'

Naseem and Brendan called over Frank Warren and Riath and told them they had agreed to work together for one fight, as long as the money could be sorted out.

But another problem had occurred to Naseem. 'What happens if it doesn't work out? If it doesn't work out with me and you, does it mean I can't train in the gym?'

'If it doesn't work out, you'll have to make arrangements with John and Dominic, because I won't be involved.'

'I want to know. Can I use the gym?'

Frank Warren intervened. 'Naz, you're creating a situation that doesn't exist at the moment. It will work out. We'll sort out Brendan's money and make sure everyone's happy and everyone knows what they've got to do.'

At eight o'clock that evening, Naseem drove to Newman Road in the Aston Martin. The gym was empty. A young girl was playing in the street outside and Naseem told her to go over the road and ask Brendan to come to the gym and to bring a headache pill and a jug of water. He had come to train.

# CHAPTER TWENTY-ONE
## The Rumblings of War

On the eve of battle, the day before 'The Full Monty', his most ambitious promotion to date, Frank Warren sipped a lunchtime beer in Sheffield and couldn't help but allow his thoughts to race ahead. However extravagant and profitable 'The Full Monty' was going to be – and it would be both – it was all but impossible for Warren not to see it as the prelude to greater events. America beckoned and the rumblings of promotional war had begun.

'Don King's going to be pissed off big-time,' said Warren. 'I like Don, but he's held Naz back in the States. I'm not happy about it and I have to do the right thing.'

Naseem's début in America had been a long time coming, so long that his frustration was even beginning to put a strain on his loyalty to Warren. For Warren, therefore, the right thing was to end his business partnership with King and to ensure that Naseem was presented to the American public by promoting him there himself.

If Naseem had been a tennis player and achieved a sufficiently high ranking, entry to the US Open would have been automatic. But a fighter's opportunities are largely beyond his control, entangled in the complexities and trade-offs of boxing politics and finance. In Naseem's case, the brake on his progress, the reason why he didn't fight in America for so long, could be traced directly to a dispute that concerned an event that had nothing to do with him: the world heavyweight title fight between Frank Bruno and Oliver McCall in 1995.

Warren's partnership with King came into effect in September 1994. It was limited to fights involving European boxers. The arrangement was that Warren would promote shows in Europe, provide the boxers he had under contract, and revenue from British television, while King would provide American television revenue through Showtime. The partnership's profits would be shared equally.

For a year, the partnership was lucrative and harmonious. Several extremely successful promotions were staged, including the wildly exciting but ultimately tragic contest between Nigel Benn and Gerald McClellan, which was watched on live television by more than thirteen million viewers. (McClellan collapsed in the ring and was rushed to the London Hospital, where he underwent brain surgery. He remains crippled, blind and barely aware of his surroundings.)

For King and Warren, the partnership was a perfect match. They made more money together than they could have done separately. Live gate receipts were generally bigger in Britain than America, and television money flowed in from ITV, and later Sky, as well as from Showtime.

Warren seemed to be one of the few people in boxing who was prepared to stick up for King. Many promoters, managers and boxers, even those who admired King's indefatigable energy and brutal intelligence, had fallen out with him, claiming to have been ripped off. But Warren was not only beguiled by King's company – for King had an exhilarating gift for making life both an adventure and entertainment – but openly expressed admiration for the partner he described as 'easily the cleverest man' he had encountered and 'the greatest promoter who ever lived'.

King was equally complimentary. When he faced trial for alleged insurance fraud in 1995, he asked Warren to move to America to run his business for him should he be imprisoned. King could also be generous. On one occasion Warren was sitting in a New York restaurant with King, who was holding a mobile phone to his ear, waiting for someone to get back to him.

'I'm ordering five Hummers,' King explained to Warren.

'What's a Hummer?'

'It's one of those trucks they developed for the Gulf War. Arnold Schwarzenegger's got one. They go through rivers and up mountains. You've got to have one.'

When the salesman came back on the phone, King said: 'Got my order? Now make that six Hummers,' and gave instructions that one was to be sent direct to Warren's Hertfordshire home. When the Hummer, which retailed at £60,000, arrived, and he discovered it could indeed go cross-country, as well as turning heads in Hertford High Street, Warren was as excited as a child with a new toy. He was less thrilled to have to pay more than a third of that sum in import duty.

King and Warren began to squabble when Frank Bruno, promoted by Warren, challenged Oliver McCall, promoted by King, for the WBC world heavyweight title. Originally, the fight was planned for the high summer of 1995, at Wembley Stadium. The terms for the Bruno–McCall fight added another layer of complexity to the partnership's arrangements. (Indeed, boxing contracts often seem to be designed to make subsequent litigation inevitable.) Warren's estimate was that if Wembley sold out, the promotion would generate a profit of $5.3 million for the partnership. The split, though, would not be 50–50. Warren's company would receive $1.5 million and King's company $3.8 million. Warren understood that if the stadium failed to sell out, those amounts would be scaled down accordingly. In addition, if Bruno won, he would then fight Mike Tyson and a sum of $2 million would be paid by King to Warren.

Warren's first irritation was at the loss of £100,000. That was the sum he put down as a non-refundable deposit to secure Wembley Stadium for a date in July 1995. The fight was postponed when it turned out that McCall had been injured in training. Warren, who had taken out insurance against the loss of the deposit, was unable to claim and lost his money.

When the fight took place in September, Bruno won, finally succeeding in his long and painful quest to become a world champion. But only 25,000 tickets were sold, far fewer than Warren originally had hoped. Afterwards, Warren met King in his suite at the Dorchester Hotel in Park Lane. King had not expected Bruno to win and was obviously unhappy. Warren anticipated some tough dealing as the shares of the profits were scaled down but he was completely unprepared for what happened. King, in full bull-elephant mode, insisted that although the promotion had not done as well as expected, he was still owed $3.8 million as a 'site fee'. A site fee is the payment casino-hotels in Las Vegas and Atlantic City make to promoters to stage big fights on their premises, and Warren could not see what relevance the term had in relation to the Wembley promotion. He became convinced that King's claim for $3.8 million was an attempt to somehow muddy the waters in the hope of avoiding the $2 million fee connected to the Tyson–Bruno fight.

The arguments that began at the Dorchester became a running sore. King would not be deflected from his demand and Warren would not concede it. Claiming to be owed $3.8 million, King subsequently withheld payments which would otherwise have been made to the partnership from a number of big fights in America, including the Tyson–Bruno fight.

The dispute inevitably wrecked a partnership that had been very profitable. Warren's explanation for what he believed was King's unreasonable behaviour, was that somehow King couldn't help it. 'It's a funny thing,' he said. 'I come from the streets and Don's from the streets. It's hard to get the streets out of you. He can't get it out of him. Everything's a hustle. He can't help it. He could have been one of the great black people of all time. He had the ability. If only he had played the game with a few people.'

The disagreement over the $3.8 million remained unresolved until January 1997, by which time Warren had decided to end the partnership when the contract expired in the following September. Warren remembers attending a late-night dinner in Nashville on 10 January at which King suggested a settlement whereby he would pay $1 million to settle all outstanding accounting issues. Warren was still unhappy but wanted to move on, so he signed a document that had already been prepared by one of King's in-house lawyers and returned to his hotel. During the night, an envelope was pushed under the door of Warren's room. He opened it, saw that it contained a copy of the document he had signed and put it back in the envelope.

Two months later, back in Britain, Warren took a closer look at the contents of the envelope. A handwritten clause, apparently extending the partnership after September 1997, had been added. According to an affidavit sworn by Warren when litigation began later in the year, the clause had been added after his signature. When Warren first saw the clause, he flew to Florida and confronted King in his palatial office at Deer Field Park, Fort Lauderdale. King said that the extension clause was on the document when Warren signed it; Warren insisted it was not. According to Warren, King then said that if Warren was not happy about an extension, it wouldn't happen. It was a 'dead issue'.

Such machinations began to have adverse effects on Naseem's career. By the beginning of 1997, by which time both Frank Bruno and Nigel Benn had retired, Naseem was Warren's biggest box-office attraction. In fighting eleven times for the Warren–King partnership, Naseem had proved he could fill arenas anywhere in Britain and that his commercial appeal extended far beyond the traditional boxing audience. The time had come to take him to America, but Warren was convinced that King, who should have facilitated Naseem's introduction to the biggest market of all, was deliberately obstructing it.

In May 1997, Showtime wanted Naseem to be on the bill when Mike Tyson fought Evander Holyfield in Las Vegas. But Warren believed that King, the promoter, blocked it. In July, when Warren was trying to negotiate a fight between Naseem and Hector Lizarraga, King, who controlled Lizarraga, demanded a purse of $500,000 for the fighter. From Warren's point of view, paying such a huge sum to a fighter who was hardly known in Britain would make it all but impossible for him to make a profit from the promotion.

Problems also arose when Warren tried to arrange a fight between Naseem and Wilfredo Vazquez, who held the WBA's version of the featherweight title. King also had Vazquez under contract, and again demanded such a large purse that the fight was financially unviable.

In August 1997, Warren wrote to King to complain that no progress was being made in putting on Naseem in America. There was no reply. Warren had already been approached by executives of HBO, the largest subscription channel in America and the arch-rival of Showtime, who screened King's promotions. During the Wimbledon tennis championships, Seth Abraham and Lou DiBella, HBO's president and vice-president, offered $2 million for the US rights to Naseem's next fight. It was far more than Showtime was paying, nevertheless, it would have broken the partnership and Warren declined. But he was losing patience with King and had become convinced that King was deliberately denying Naseem exposure in America because he knew he could make more money by not involving the partnership and exclusively putting his own fighters on Showtime. Warren was also aware that since King realised the partnership was coming to an end, he had no interest in furthering Naseem's career.

Warren reopened negotiations with HBO in August. King found out and left a message on Warren's answerphone, accusing him of 'jumping ship'. Warren replied in writing, saying he had been pushed overboard.

HBO offered $1.7 million for Naseem to fight Kevin Kelley, a former world featherweight champion they had under contract. The Kelley fight would be the first instalment of a six-fight deal worth $12 million, as long as Naseem kept winning; Warren booked Madison Square Garden for 19 December, at a cost of $750,000 for the evening; and King, who was indeed 'pissed off big-time' as Warren predicted, planned his riposte. It would not be long coming.

For Warren, on the eve of The Full Monty in Sheffield, even the fulfilment of a long-held ambition to put on a show made up of nothing but title fights, all scheduled for the full twelve-round distance, was somehow secondary to what lay ahead. The Sheffield Arena was sold out, pay-per-view sales were far better than for the Hardy fight and two world title fights, Naseem against Jose Badillo and Joe Calzaghe against Chris Eubank, would be a fitting climax. But it was still a side-show compared with Madison Square Garden and Warren versus King.

For Brendan, the Sheffield promotion was an end in itself. It marked the culmination of his life's work in the city. That thought had been poignantly brought home to him forty-eight hours before the first bell of a very long evening, as he once again waited for Naseem to arrive in the steam room of the Swallow Hotel. An old acquaintance, a scrap-metal merchant named Colin Lake, greeted Brendan through the heat and mist. Lake had sat next to Brendan at the Cutler's Hall, on the night that Naseem had his first fight as an amateur.

'You know what, Brendan?' said Lake. 'All those years ago, you used to say that one day you'd bring a European title fight to Sheffield. And we all laughed at you. We all said that pigs might fly.'

'Yeah, I remember.'

As well as the two world title fights, The Full Monty featured a world title eliminator, a European title fight and two British title fights. Brendan originally had six fighters on the bill, but Paul Griffin pulled out injured, which left five: Naseem, Ryan Rhodes, Johnny Nelson, Pele Reid and John Keeton.

It was five weeks since Brendan had told Naseem he wouldn't train him any more, only to relent at the crisis meeting. Relations had been patched up, but there had been further arguments between Brendan and Riath about how much Brendan would be paid. It was Frank Warren who achieved the limited reconciliation which ensured that Brendan would train Naseem and work as his second in the corner. Warren even offered to make up the difference of £5,000 between Riath's final offer and Brendan's minimum demand.

With the King dispute erupting, Warren could have done without rows in the camp, but he knew how important it was to keep Brendan and Naseem together. 'You know what I do? I manage everybody,' said Warren on the day before The Full Monty. What he meant was that he listened to moans, provided personal counselling, massaged egos, patched up disputes and tried to keep the show on the road.

Warren could have been an agony aunt. In a way he was. 'Brendan trusts me and Naz trusts me. I would hate to see them break up. I never really thought there would be a split. There was a lot of posturing on both sides. It was like a husband and wife not talking to each other – tell him his dinner's on the table. But Naz knows Brendan's value and Brendan knows Naz's value. Boxing is a funny business. When kids start out, they say they'll be with you for ever, be loyal, but as they get older they assess the situation differently, and you can understand that. They're the guys who get in the ring, and it can lead to rifts. The name of the game is to keep things going.'

It was just as well Warren did, and it was just as well that although Naseem trained only for a little over a month, he trained hard, because Naseem's opponent, Jose Badillo, was the kind of boxer it could be fatal to take too lightly.

Brendan saw the danger signs when he watched a video recording of the only fight Badillo had lost in twenty-one appearances, a world title challenge against Tom Johnson in December 1995. Johnson built a big points lead but was twice knocked down late in the fight and was fortunate to hang on to win. As far as Brendan was concerned, Badillo was as good as unbeaten. He was a southpaw, a big puncher, and, as became evident when Badillo arrived in Sheffield, his face was virtually unmarked, his nose unbroken – another indication of quality.

Badillo trained in a newly opened gym near the centre of Sheffield. Little did he know that it belonged to Brendan, and that its manager, a young Anglo-Indian named Dave Caldwell, was one of Brendan's boxers. Caldwell made himself very helpful to Badillo, his manager, trainer and sparring partners, opening the gym whenever they needed it, and hanging around to watch sparring before tidying up when they left. His reports confirmed Brendan's impressions. Badillo was a class fighter, fast and good on his feet, always ready to set himself to hit and especially quick to counter with the left hand.

Brendan's instructions to Naseem were given over several days and repeated as he bandaged his hands before the fight. All the boxers from St Thomas's used the same dressing room in the bowels of the arena. John Keeton had been out first, had given a good account of himself, but lost. All the others had won, Pele Reid with a struggle, Ryan Rhodes and Johnny Nelson brilliantly. Only one was left to fight: Naseem.

'You've got to go back to what you did against Belcastro,' said Brendan. 'Stay southpaw and torment him with the lead right hand. Just use single shots to begin with, bust him up, break his nose, close his eyes. Don't use combinations, and don't have a war with him, because he's too dangerous. Hit him from all angles, but single shots.

You'll start breaking him up by the fifth round. Then you can open up and take him out.'

Naseem listened all right. He never boxed more carefully or effectively. In the first round, he set out his stall with the right-hand jab, spearing Badillo to the face and even showing him one of his old party tricks – looking at the opponent's feet and hitting him in the face. In the second round the jabs came in doubles, triples, quadruples, most of them finding the mark. By the third, Badillo was cut and banged up. By the fourth, the evil smile had appeared on Naseem's face. In the fifth, Naseem put on a display of shuffling and posing, cut short because the round lasted two minutes instead of three. Perhaps the timekeeper disapproved. In the sixth, Badillo had his only successes: two left hooks that caught Naseem to the head. By the seventh, Badillo was taking a hammering. His face was a terrible mess when his corner flung a towel across the ring and the referee called a halt.

Now the announcement could be made officially. Warren confirmed that the next stop would be Madison Square Garden. He didn't care what Don King thought about it, and yes, the next opponent would in all probability be Kevin Kelley, who just happened to be at ringside, obligingly trading boasts and insults with Naseem.

With the Sheffield crowd cheering to the last, and all his boxers safe, Brendan had enjoyed his greatest night in boxing. He still spared a thought for Badillo. 'That's the sad part. He's finished as a fighter.'

# CHAPTER TWENTY-TWO

## Like a Hole in the Head

Brendan should never have gone to Los Angeles. Afterwards, he brooded for two weeks and the pain he had suffered there grew worse.

Eleven days after The Full Monty, the World Boxing Organisation held its annual convention in Los Angeles. Frank Warren, the leading promoter allied to the WBO, took with him Naseem, his prize champion, as well as a group of his other boxers, including Joe Calzaghe, who had won the WBO super-middleweight title by beating Chris Eubank, and Ryan Rhodes, who was hoping for a crack at the middleweight title.

Brendan didn't really need to go to Los Angeles at all. He was Ryan Rhodes's manager but there was no need for Brendan to lobby for Rhodes to get a shot at the title. Rhodes's claims were always likely to be met – not so much on the merits of his case but because it suited Warren, who was the WBO's main promoter and therefore its biggest provider of income through sanction fees. But he went anyway, buying his own ticket and soon regretting it; for him it was a terrible trip.

It began with a scuffle near the Virgin Airways check-in desk at Terminal 3, Heathrow Airport. The miscreants were Naseem and Chris Eubank, who had turned up not to fly but to have a word with Frank Warren about future fights. There was bad blood, long term and short term, between Naseem and Eubank. The long term went back years, to the time when Eubank had spent a few days at Brendan's gym, sparring with Herol Graham. Eubank saw the young Naseem leap into the St Thomas's ring by vaulting the top rope and later incorporated the move into his own routine. When Naseem himself turned pro and started jumping over the ropes, people assumed he was copying Eubank, so Naseem told the world that Eubank had stolen the trick from him. What Naseem didn't admit was that he had also copied it, from Ryan Rhodes, who was the true originator.

The more recent needle between Naseem and Eubank was equally inconsequential. Eubank had been a late addition to The Full Monty but had rather stolen the show. Sky's pre-fight publicity concentrated on Eubank, and Eubank's fight with Joe Calzaghe followed Naseem's, as if it was top of the bill. Theatrically, Sky was right, for Eubank's showmanship carried more conviction than Naseem's. Where Naseem's pre-fight boasting tended to be tiresome and predictable, Eubank's always contained a hint of self-mockery and a *frisson* of the unexpected. His presence was more amusing and intriguing than Naseem's. Eubank, of course, wasn't half the boxer, and on the night Naseem won and Eubank was beaten, but as a performer Naseem had been upstaged and he knew it.

The Battle of Heathrow, or 'The Big Flight,' as the *Sun* called it in their front-page report the following morning, was a juvenile exchange, too ludicrous to be reprehensible. Pride and envy, two of the seven deadly sins, were chiefly to blame. Eubank, dressed, as was his custom, as a short-sighted eighteenth-century plantation owner, with jodhpurs, cane and monocle, was the centre of attention in the terminal, surrounded by autograph hunters.

Naseem, who was receiving less public attention, called across to Eubank, asking how come he hadn't any championship belts. Modern world championship belts are as tawdry as the novelties in cheap Christmas crackers, but for boxers they have symbolic value. Naseem held his WBO and IBF world championship belts aloft and invited Eubank to come over and take a look at them. Eubank approached, grabbed the belts and hurled them across the floor. Naseem threw a punch which caught Eubank on the chin, at which point Frank Warren stepped between them.

Twelve hours and more than 5,000 miles later, Brendan was on the receiving end of Naseem's displeasure, and it hurt him badly. Transport had been laid on to take Frank Warren's party from the Los Angeles International Airport to the Sheraton Hotel, the convention venue. Warren, Brendan, Naseem, Ryan Rhodes and Joe Calzaghe rode together in a stretch limousine.

Naseem began with an old tease, a wind-up. 'What did you win, Brendan? Nothing. You never even won an area title.'

'Listen, if you'd had to do it the way I did, you'd never have lasted, getting up at four in the morning and running before going to work for ten or twelve hours and then training after work. You'd never have done it.'

After several minutes, to and fro, Naseem went in to wound: 'You know your trouble, Brendan? You never stood up to anybody. You never stood up to anybody in your life. You always let people bully you. Like that time with Mickey Duff when he slagged you off and you just stood for it.'

Before Brendan could answer, Warren, who sensed trouble, once again intervened as the peacemaker. 'You two are worse than a married couple, now shut up.'

But the damage had been done. Brendan became obsessed by what Naseem had said, as if Naseem had stained his whole life. He knew what he'd wanted to say in reply: that he'd left Dublin for Sheffield when he was eighteen, that he'd made his own way, done his own thing, that he'd married an English woman, a Protestant, and not one of his family had been at the wedding; and that Naseem, by contrast, was controlled by his family, that he let Riath and the others manipulate and monopolise him. How would Naseem have coped with getting barred in the amateurs? How would he have coped with Herol Graham and all that hassle? So how dare Naseem say he'd never stood up to anybody?

They were poisonous thoughts that Brendan allowed to fester in his head for the three days of the convention. While Naseem, Frank Warren and the others flew on to New York to publicise the Kevin Kelley fight, Brendan flew home alone. He had eleven hours to sit and think with no one to deflect or diffuse his ruminations. By the time he arrived at Heathrow, Brendan wished he'd grabbed Naseem in the limousine and tried to hit him.

There was a conscious, rational explanation for the awful intensity of

Brendan's reaction. Naseem should never have attacked him like that in front of others, especially in front of Joe Calzaghe, whom Brendan hardly knew. And what Naseem had said was horribly unfair. But – and here was the deepest hurt and the most difficult part to admit – there was truth in it. Brendan had not stood up for himself. But the person he had failed to stand up to was not Mickey Duff, or indeed any of the others who had given him trouble over the years. It was Naseem. Brendan had allowed himself to be bullied by the bully he had in part created. And perhaps, even, that was what Naseem had been trying to say – that deep down he wished Brendan had stood up to him.

Naseem returned to Sheffield two weeks later, walking into the gym on the evening of 10 November. He hadn't trained for a month and there was just over five weeks to go before the Kelley fight at Madison Square Garden. If he wanted to be really fit for the fight, he was already cutting it fine. Naseem did a light workout and that evening went to the Swallow Hotel to use a running machine. Brendan gave Naseem a massage in the steam room, acting quite normally, making small talk. But he had a plan. Frank Warren was coming to Sheffield in a few days. Brendan would tell Warren what he was going to do, and then he would tell Naseem.

In fact, events moved more quickly. The next day, his second day back in the gym, Naseem did ten rounds on the light and heavy punch-bags and was scintillating. Brendan could hardly believe what he was watching. It was all but impossible that someone could walk in after a month's break and perform so well. A few of the other boxers who were finishing their work stopped and watched in astonishment. They had seen it before, but it was still amazing. They were watching a phenomenon and they knew it. So did Brendan. Then the thought struck him: what better time would there ever be than now?

Brendan waited until the gym had cleared. Naseem had a shower and Brendan brought him a jug of iced water.

'Naz, I've got something to say to you. I've said it before, but don't think I don't mean it. I don't want to work with you any more. I'm not chucking you out of the gym, but I don't want to work with you any more. You can work with John or Dominic, whatever, but I want out.'

'Why?'

'I won't give you a reason. But you and me are finished.'

Brendan wanted no discussion. He left Naseem getting changed and walked across the road to his house.

'You know what, Alma?' he said. 'I've just gone and sacked myself from the best fighter in the world.'

Brendan went upstairs, lay on his bed reading for a while and had a bath. Soon after nine o'clock, he heard voices downstairs. Alma was telling someone to come in. At first Brendan thought it must be Naseem. He knew Naseem had been shocked, even if he couldn't have been entirely surprised, and that he would have driven home in his Ferrari and tried to work out what to do.

But it wasn't Naseem. 'Brendan, it's Naz's father,' said Alma, who had come upstairs. 'He wants to see you and he's right upset.'

Brendan dressed and went down.

'I don't want anyone else to train Naz,' said Sal. 'What's gone wrong, Brendan? What's happened?'

Brendan listed his grievances. His money had been cut from 25 per cent, to 16 per cent and then, by his calculation, to 4 per cent. And for the last fight, in Sheffield, Riath had offered him £30,000 and he'd had to fight to get it up to £45,000. He'd been ripped off.

'I want you to train him,' said Sal Hamed.

'Sal, I've had enough. He's insulted me in the car with Frank Warren and Joe Calzaghe there. He doesn't know what I've had to go through. I don't want to know.'

'I won't have him being disrespectful to you,' said Sal. 'That was wrong. But we must work something out. Can he at least train in the gym?'

'Yes, but John will train him. And he'll have to sort out what John will get paid.'

Sal left, still unhappy, and insisting that he wanted Brendan to train Naseem.

The next day, Naseem trained, John Ingle supervised and Brendan sat on his steps and watched. He would not even speak to Naseem. Naseem came over for Brendan to tie the laces of his gloves but neither said a word. For eleven days, Naseem was trained by John and Dominic, and Brendan watched, silently. Each day, Naseem's father and brothers, Riath, Nabeel, Murad and Ali, most of whom hardly ever went to the gym, turned up to watch Naseem train and to lend moral support. One afternoon, one of the youngest boxers asked: 'What's happening, Brendan? There's a terrible atmosphere in the gym.'

Naseem broke the impasse by ringing Brendan on a Sunday evening, 23 November.

'I want to see you, Brendan. Can I come down with my dad and Riath?'

'Don't bring Riath. I'll talk to you and your dad. I'll see you in the gym at nine o'clock.'

The meeting, held in the centre of the gym with three wooden chairs drawn up in a circle on the wooden floor, lasted two hours. The most important contribution came from Naseem. Brendan complained that he had been ripped off and that he was entitled to 25 per cent; Naseem insisted he'd been young and inexperienced and should never have agreed to 25 per cent in the first place. Brendan complained about what Naseem had said in front of others in the car in Los Angeles; Naseem apologised and promised it wouldn't happen again. Brendan said that Dominic would train Naseem while Brendan watched and passed on observations; Naseem replied that he only wanted one person to train him, Brendan, that they had been together for sixteen years. Brendan said he didn't want Riath and the other brothers to come into the gym; Naseem and his father agreed, but asked that Nabeel should be allowed in with his video camera. Brendan accepted. Finally, Brendan said he wanted 10 per cent of Naseem's purse against Kevin Kelley as a trainer's fee; Naseem and his father agreed and all shook hands.

Now Naseem could train properly and without upset. But there were two days less than four weeks to go before he was due to get into the ring at Madison Square Garden for the most important fight of his life.

Once again Brendan had gone to the brink, looked over, and retreated. He was finding that however strongly he felt that Naseem had mistreated him, it was almost impossible to break away. Whatever had happened between them, he didn't want to see Naseem licked. He didn't want Naseem to fight at Madison Square Garden, his first fight abroad, without being in the corner. And although he might and did say that he needed Naseem and all the hassle like a hole in the head, he still needed him.

# Riath Hamed's Story

*Naz doesn't remember it because it never really affected him, but we suffered a lot from racism in the early days. There were bricks through our windows, pellet guns shooting at the windows and NF sprayed on our windows and doors.*

*Our school was racist as well. Every day it was you Paki, you Black Bastard. The teachers didn't seem interested in us and they were always putting us down. I left school at fifteen, with no qualifications. My dad had this idea of me going into education to be a doctor or lawyer. I went to college and went on to get a degree, a 2.1 in political and social science. The teachers at the college were bohemians and socialists. They never had an ounce of racism and it was a breath of fresh air for me to be unleashed into an atmosphere where you could be creative.*

*After university, I worked with the Yemeni community as a voluntary worker, and then for the local education department and the health authority, translating. Then, one night in 1995, Naz and I sat up for hours talking about the future and his career, and a couple of days later he said he wanted me to work for him as his business manager. At first, I didn't really want to do it, to be in the boxing game, but he said he would rather have me than anyone dodgy handling his affairs, and he said he would explain everything as we went along.*

*When I started as Naz's business manager, there was nothing in place apart from one or two sponsorships in the pipeline, such as the Sony and Joe Bloggs contracts. I developed those with John Ingle. Brendan and John might say something different, but I've got to the stage in my life where there's no point in telling lies.*

157

*I'm caught in the middle between Naseem and Brendan. I'll always respect Brendan as a trainer because he's incredibly good at what he does. I put him on a pedestal as someone I respect enormously for his contribution to boxing and to Naseem's life. But he's never really managed Naseem. Brendan always feels he's been done, he's been robbed, that he's a victim. When you put up an argument that he hasn't really managed Naseem and isn't entitled to 25 per cent of what Naseem earns, Brendan turns it round and says that Naz would not exist without him, that by the time he turned professional, Naz was ready-made. But Brendan has no right to say he's made Naz. He may have enhanced and nurtured his talent, but no one apart from the Creator can say 'I made this person'. So when Brendan once said to me that he had done the hard job, and that I was feeding off his rewards, I saw him for what he was. He uses emotional tactics to try to make people feel guilty. There's a constant battering of his philosophies. Some people believe it, but some people resent it.*

*Brendan thinks he knows Naseem inside out but in fact Naseem knows Brendan inside out and he knows what's happening. It hurts Brendan so much that I'm in a position to negotiate what he gets from Naseem, and that I'm the only person Naseem will talk to about his finances. Brendan feels that I'm interfering, that I've come from nowhere and I've stolen his investment. He's done unspeakable things to try to degrade me and put me down, and now he won't acknowledge me. He won't even look me in the face. He sees me as the person who has blocked and diluted his investment. But I don't hate Brendan. I never would.*

*What hurts me even more is that it's all down to money. I idolised Brendan as a kid, growing up and going down to the gym. We used to have arguments about religion, socialism and capitalism but now our history together is meaningless. As a kid, Brendan was always there for us. Now, when he walks straight past me as if I don't exist, it hurts. But he really believes it all, that black is white and white is black, and he won't change his mind however right and just your argument is. That's why I found it so hard to negotiate with him.*

*The poison all came in after 1995 when I started working for Naz. To begin with, Brendan told Naz that getting me on board was the best thing he'd ever done. But now I'm the big, bad wolf because Brendan's lost control of the finances. I think Brendan wanted to take control of everything, all Naz's business, to make him a Brendan Ingle entity. But I've taken all that away.*

*Brendan didn't let Naz grow up. He feels so hurt now because in his own mind he feels he's lost Naseem. When a father loses control of his child, he feels he's lost something he's brought into this world. But that's life. Brendan has never understood that.*

*I'd like to sit Brendan down and shake him, tell him to wake up, to stop being like this, to tell him that there comes a time in everyone's life when the payback is over. He told Naseem when he was twelve or even younger that he wanted 25 per cent of his earnings for life. How unfair is that? Who has a concept of money at that age? That's why I say it was all about money, and that's why I'm seen as the block on Brendan's investment.*

*What Brendan has never appreciated is that I'm in Naseem's family and that we are all incredibly close. In our minds, what blood is, what families are, is everything. Naseem is still our little brother. That's why I get so nervous at his fights that I can't even talk. It's not that I doubt him, it's just that I wish that every punch he takes was on me. I'd rather take the pain than see him hurt because I love him so much. We all do, and when he comes into the house, it's the same as it always was. There's no special treatment, no fame. He can't live without the family and the family can't live without him.*

*I've made so much money for Naseem. I don't go around shouting about it, but it equals what he's made out of boxing. The two amounts, what he's made in the ring and outside it, are about level. They stack up well together. Brendan could never have done anything like that. And I don't take 25 per cent. I would never make those ludicrous demands.*

*The arguments with Brendan have been going on for some time. It's all so tiring and petty. I'm sick of it and I want it to come out. The reason I'm saying all this is that I don't give a fuck any more, I don't care whether Brendan will read this or not. I want my feelings to be on the record, so that people can make up their own minds.*

# CHAPTER TWENTY-THREE
## New York, New York

Brendan faced a sea of faces, a battery of cameras and blinding lights. His moment had come. Two hundred people – reporters, photographers, cameramen and technicians – crammed into a room that was much too small. They were hot; winter coats were off and brows being wiped. It wasn't the audience that mattered to Brendan, but the venue. For if The Full Monty marked the fulfilment of his life in Sheffield, he now stood at the entrance to his dreams. The low-ceilinged ante-room allocated for the final press conference before Naseem's contest against Kevin Kelley might not be the main arena, but Brendan had arrived at boxing's Mecca, La Scala and Acropolis. He was in Madison Square Garden.

'Let me tell you about this fella,' Brendan began. 'I saw him when he was seven years of age, a little kid, and he came down the gym seven days a week. I says, me and you are going to make a fortune, if you listen.'

Brendan had planned to make a speech as soon as he heard where the press conference was to be. He hadn't written down or worked out what he was going to say because when it came to public speaking he always trusted that the words would come, and they always did. He was certainly proving better at grabbing and holding attention than any of the monotone speakers who preceded him, including Frank Warren and Lou DiBella, the vice-president of HBO. Brendan had a surer sense of theatre. The others had leaned forward and conversed with their microphones. Brendan had stood up, taken off his jacket, ignored the microphone and thrown his voice to the back, like an actor of the old school.

'We went around all the pit villages, the mining villages in Yorkshire, the north of England, right down to the Midlands, and he kept winning. As an amateur, he lost five contests. Except he didn't lose. He got robbed. Because he could box that way, orthodox' – Brendan clenched his fists and adopted the orthodox position – 'he could box that way, southpaw' – he demonstrated southpaw – 'he could switch; he could stand square; he could box from the side. And you couldn't hit him. That's five ways I teach, and he's got it off to an art.'

While Brendan demonstrated the five ways of boxing and held his audience in thrall, Naseem, next to Brendan on the dais, faced the New York media with his elbows on the table, his chin resting in his hands, resolutely staring to the front, with no smile or turn of the head to endorse Brendan's words. Perhaps he feared what Brendan might say, that he might be indiscreet. Brendan was perfectly capable of using such an occasion to make public his grievances, to shock the world with accusations of being ripped off and mistreated. But Naseem had no need to worry, and nor did Riath, who stood away to one side, wondering what Brendan, the loose cannon, might choose to detonate. Brendan was just playing the game, helping ticket sales by playing the stage Irishman for all he was worth and charming the socks off his audience.

'Nobody's done him any favours and certainly nobody's done me any favours, because the amateurs barred me twenty years ago. But I said I would bring someone who's world champion to the home of boxing, Madison Square Garden, and brother we're here.'

It was coming up to Christmas in New York City and Naseem seemed bigger than Santa Claus. The canyons of Manhattan usually summon a sense of wonder in visitors who would not be surprised if Superman flew in. Now the face of Naseem Hamed, the Arab kid from Sheffield who had never even boxed in America, was twenty-two feet high on the best-placed billboard in Times Square. At the entrance to the Lincoln Tunnel linking Manhattan Island to New Jersey, it was bigger. All over the city, on bus stops and telephone kiosks, in every newspaper, advertisements for the fight portrayed Naseem pouting and reclining against a leopardskin background, *à la* Marilyn Monroe, arms outstretched, with flames issuing from his boxing gloves. The image, part photo, part montage, was the creation of David LaChappelle, one of America's most fashionable and expensive photographers. The charge for his photo session was $125,000, a fair slice of the $1.7 million HBO had allocated for an advertising campaign concentrated in but not limited to New York. On Sunset Boulevard in Hollywood, a twenty-two-storey-high poster of Naseem had been erected, which, as one paper put it, 'was more than Gloria Swanson ever got'.

When Naseem's turn came at the press conference, his purpose was to intimidate Kelley. He chose his standard approach: humiliation. Wearing a green silk bomber jacket, and leaning forward to the microphone, he spoke with a smirk.

'I've been here two minutes, basically, and I've taken over boxing. If Kelley came to my home town and he took over all the publicity, and I was on the outside looking in, I'd be sick. I'd be absolutely sick. And that's what's happened. He's supposed to be a great featherweight and he's from New York, but I haven't seen him anywhere. I've been doing interviews all week. I've been all over the billboards. He's allowed me to come all the way over from England and steal the show.'

It was indeed true that Kelley, who was known as an accomplished and unstoppable self-publicist, had been invisible until he turned up for the press conference; so invisible that Frank Warren introduced him as the Scarlet Pimpernel. But Kelley's three-week sojourn in a training camp in the Pocono Mountains in Pennsylvania was time well spent. He knew full well that in the promotional script he was cast as the fall-guy. He knew that HBO had not spent $1.7 million plastering the city with Naseem's face to see him defeated. Kelley's role was to talk a good fight and get beaten. But he wasn't inclined to play his part and when he did arrive in New York, he was smouldering with resentment and more than ready to fight.

'First things first,' said Kelley, spitting out the words, and especially the names, in his anger. 'The only person I'm thinking of is Hamed. Because the bottom line is he came here and he thinks he's all that he says he is. I'm going to show him that he's not. I want to thank Frank Warren for bringing him, but when I'm hitting him, Warren's going to say "You're beating up, my money, Kev." And HBO's going to feel

162

the same, that I'm beating their money up. And that's exactly what I'm going to do. Every time I land, their pockets are going to feel it.

'I'm here because I'm a fighter first and an entertainer second. Hamed is an entertainer first, a fighter second. One big difference the media have missed. When he hits them, they get up. When I hit them, they're unconscious. Nobody can knock me out and Hamed, I've got news for you. You're not the hardest-punching featherweight. I am.'

Naseem had known for years, and had said soon after turning professional, that one day he would meet 'kids who could really fight' and that he would need heart and courage as well as skill to pull him through. And when he met the real good kids, he would have to beat them mentally. Kelley was a real good kid, and he showed all the signs of being every bit as tough, mentally and physically, as Naseem. Indeed when they stood nose to nose for the photographs that accompanied the 'War of Words' headlines in the New York tabloids the next day – which, as intended, produced a late rush for tickets – it was noticeable that Kelley looked the bigger man.

But although Naseem and Kelley glared at each other in the approved manner, and had delighted Frank Warren and HBO by their promises of violence, the press conference was Brendan's show and it was left to him to issue the call to arms.

'On Friday night, you're going to see a fantastic fight because that man there, Kevin Kelley, he's a champion and a fighter of class. He's beaten champions and fighters of class. The papers this week are saying how can you compare Naseem with Muhammad Ali? Quite simple: Muhammad Ali was his idol and certainly my idol. I got up at three in the morning when he boxed, to watch him in the cinema, on television. Brilliant orthodox fighter, could shuffle. Naseem can box five ways, he can shuffle, back-flip, forward roll, hit you from any angle and take you out.

'Fellow says, how would you class him? I says well, if you break his hands, he'll kick you. If you break his feet, he'll bite you. If you pull out his teeth, he'll hit you with his head. So you think he's a dirty fighter? No, he's not a dirty fighter. He's a clean fighter. What I'm saying to you, Kevin Kelley, is that to beat him on Friday night, you're going to have to nail him to the floor. So all those people like myself who followed the boxing through the forties and fifties at the Mecca of boxing, Madison Square Garden, be here, and don't blink because you're in for a hell of a fight.'

Brendan and Naseem had arrived at the John F. Kennedy International Airport during the night of Monday 8 December, eleven days before the fight. Brendan had one piece of luggage, Naseem forty-one. Three days later, Brendan, who had supervised the setting up of the training arrangements, left his son John in charge and flew back across the Atlantic to be chief cornerman when Ryan Rhodes fought for the WBO world middleweight title in Sheffield. Naseem had been at ringside for every fight in Rhodes's professional career. They were best mates, after all. But Ryan had his big chance six days before Naseem's fight at Madison Square Garden, and Naseem had to follow Ryan's fight by listening to Sky's television commentary, relayed by telephone to his suite on the 47th floor of the New York Palace hotel.

Most of the eight members of Naseem's entourage managed to find an extension to listen to the fight. Naseem had the phone in the sitting room. John Ingle lay on Naseem's bed on another extension. Nabeel Hamed had the phone in the bathroom, and the others were spread around the entrance hall, dining area and kitchen.

Rhodes's Canadian opponent, Otis Grant, was a clever and accomplished boxer. For most of the fight, Grant held the upper hand, but in the later rounds Rhodes was evidently the stronger. He might win by stopping Grant, and everyone in Naseem's suite was urging him on as if they were at ringside. But the big punch never landed and when the judges' scores were counted up, Grant had won decisively.

Naseem was quiet for a few moments. He put down the phone. 'Come on,' he said. 'We're going training.'

Naseem led the party downstairs and into the minibus that was laid on to take them to the gymnasium. Naseem was subdued and when someone in the back of the bus cracked a joke, he scowled. Ryan had lost and it wasn't the time for laughs.

John Ingle, supervising in Brendan's absence, put Naseem in to spar with Kevin Adamson, a middleweight, and Clifton Mitchell, a heavyweight who only a year earlier had fought for the European title. The idea was to make Naseem work for every minute of every round. He sparred a minute against Adamson, then switched immediately to Mitchell when John called 'change'. It was supposed to be body-sparring, no headguards and no shots to the head, but since Mitchell was a full foot taller than Naseem, there was always likely to be the odd punch that went astray. In the fifth round, Clifton caught Naseem flush in the face with a right-hand punch. Blood began to trickle from one of his nostrils. Naseem took a step back and stopped boxing. He asked Kevin Adamson to get out of the ring, and wiped his nose with his glove. Clifton knew what was coming, and he did his best to cover up and hold Naseem off. But he took a pasting. For a round and a half, Naseem bashed the heavyweight to body and head, bloodying his nose and face, until John shouted 'that's enough!' and pulled them out.

Naseem's anger was impressive, but it was also worrying that he had been affected, even disturbed, by Ryan's defeat. Indeed, Naseem said he wouldn't accept that Ryan had really lost until he saw a video of the fight. 'Ryan's basically a bigger version of me,' Naseem said. For Ryan to lose without being knocked out or stopped was unthinkable. It should have been impossible.

On the afternoon of Monday 15 December – with four days left to the fight – the minibus taking Naseem and his entourage from their headquarters at the New York Palace to the Blue Velvet gym was jam-packed. As well as John Ingle, the sparring partners and Naseem's brothers, Brendan had flown back from London, and Johnny Nelson had come with him. As the minibus lurched south down Seventh Avenue, the driver kept pace with the traffic lights and yellow cabs by alternately accelerating flat out and standing on the brakes. Naseem sat in the front passenger seat, not bothering with the seatbelt. He turned the heater up high and fiddled with the radio until he found the music he wanted and turned it up full blast. 'Hey Johnny,' he shouted to Johnny Nelson in the back of the bus as it charged through Times Square, 'Cop a look at me on that poster!' Naseem was in the best of moods. He had managed to put Ryan Rhodes's defeat behind him and today was a big day because Michael Jackson, fellow-celebrity and, Naseem liked to think, friend, was coming to the gym to watch him train.

In the Blue Velvet gym, the ground floor of a dirty pre-war building on a decaying street near Gramercy Park, John took Naseem on the pads while Brendan sat alone by the side of the ring. Brendan often liked to keep an eye on what was going on, to watch people from a distance, but this was not St Thomas's. The place was throbbing with music, by Naseem's command, so loud that speech was difficult. Brendan was a forgotten figure, redundant. In his left hand he held a small travelling alarm clock and called out time at the end of each round, but Naseem and John mostly didn't hear him.

A twitchy, rake-thin man who looked like Malcolm X entered and quickly toured the gym, eyes darting, before returning to the door. All apparently clear. Michael Jackson, who had been waiting for the signal in his private, dark-windowed bus, was spirited inside. The door was instantly locked behind him. He was dressed entirely in black except for white socks, and wore a black hat, and a mask that covered his nose and mouth, making him conspicuous and instantly recognisable. He removed it to reveal skin that was ghostly but dirty white, with the texture of parchment.

Jackson's arrival had been noticed in the street, and a crowd had gathered outside the gym, faces pressed against the glass doors. Naseem stopped his work and climbed down from the ring to greet Jackson, and to introduce him to Riath and Nabeel. After a brief conversation, Naseem returned to the ring and resumed on the pads. Jackson, spectating, stood by himself, leaning against the ring-apron and tapping the canvas with his hand to the beat of the music as Naseem demonstrated every shuffle, switch and step in his repertoire.

Riath, who had come to watch training for the first time in a week, having been laid low with a cold, engaged Jackson in conversation. Riath had bought a pair of steel worry balls, which he moved around in his hand in the manner of Humphrey Bogart in *The Caine Mutiny*. Jackson may have been impressed, but Brendan was not. 'What does he

166

need those for?' Brendan said subsequently. 'He's just trying to draw attention to himself. He wants people to go up to him and ask him why he's got them.'

Jackson disappeared as he had arrived, like a spectre, leaving Riath to reveal that 'Michael said Naz moved better than any boxer he's seen since Muhammad Ali. In fact, he said Naz reminds him a hundred per cent of Ali.'

The comparison with Ali, first made years before by Brendan, kept recurring. One of the house trainers at the Blue Velvet, Buddy McGirt, who was welterweight world champion at the beginning of the 1990s, observed Naseem for several sessions and concluded: 'Hamed is awesome. He does things that are unbelievable, like a young Ali.'

Naseem sometimes went further, claiming to be Ali's superior. Early in the year, when he was invited by a magazine to nominate the three best boxers of the past thirty years, Naseem placed himself first, Muhammad Ali second and Sugar Ray Leonard third. His explanation: 'I'm going to retire undefeated, a living legend with all the belts. I know I've got something a lot of fighters haven't got. I've got God on my side. Both Ali and Leonard lost a few times, but I just can't see myself getting beaten.'

Such allusions and illusions were too much for some. When Seth Abraham, the president of HBO, introduced Naseem to the New York press as 'a combination of the Beatles and Muhammad Ali', Wally Matthews of the *New York Post*, a noted wise-guy, wrote that 'so far, Hamed fights about as well as Ringo Starr and I doubt he sings as well as Ali'.

Similar scepticism was expressed by Carlos Ortiz, a great Puerto Rican fighter who held a world title for most of the 1960s. Ortiz watched Naseem train and walked away shaking his head. 'You call that sparring? It looks like dancing to me. I can't make this kid out at all.'

Frank Warren stood on the tenth floor of the New York Palace, gazing across the Christmas bustle of Madison Avenue to St Patrick's

Cathedral. He was at the threshold of a defining episode in his life and was in reflective mood. 'I've always been a restless person,' he said. 'But for me, success means peace of mind, knowing that your family is well provided for. Sometimes I'm tempted to give all this up, to walk away from promoting, from business. I wouldn't miss it.'

The restless side of Warren had taken him from a council flat in Islington with a view over the back of King's Cross station to a four-room suite in the heart of Manhattan. It had taken him in seventeen years from his first promotions, seedy, unlicensed brawls held in the old Rainbow cinema at Finsbury Park in north London, to the ultimate: Madison Square Garden.

If Warren was really seeking peace of mind, he had chosen a strange approach, unless he was determined to meet every challenge and beat off every enemy before riding into the sunset. He was promoting three major shows, all headed by world title fights, in Sheffield, London and New York, within a week. To accommodate his promotional team for the New York operation alone, including fighters, publicity staff, boxing officials and his own TV unit, he had reserved 200 rooms in four hotels. His resources were stretched to breaking point and he was crossing the ocean, mostly by Concorde, as often as crossing the street.

Don King, the partner turned number one villain, had been repulsed for the moment. King's response to Warren's defection had been to call a press conference at the Mirage casino-hotel in Las Vegas in November, after the world heavyweight title fight between Evander Holyfield and Michael Moorer, for the express purpose of launching a tirade against 'the traitor', Warren. King declared he had loved Warren and that he had come to Warren's aid on his deathbed (he sent a get-well telegram to the hospital after Warren was shot); that he had raised him 'from destitution and ill-repute to high esteem and stature in the boxing world' and that Warren was like Judas, except that his reward had been greater than thirty pieces of silver. King even claimed that Naseem had wanted King to promote him rather than Warren. 'Naseem told me that Frank never had the power to take him to the top, but I told him to stay with Frank,' King said. Naseem was quick to deny King's claim. King had been stung not merely by what he saw as

Warren's desertion, but by his alliance with HBO, the rivals of King's subscription channel, Showtime, and by his decision to promote in New York, which was a direct provocation to King on his own turf.

As well as flinging invective, King sued Warren in the English High Court for alleged breach of their partnership contract. The first round of a protracted legal battle was the seeking by King of an injunction to prevent Warren's Madison Square Garden promotion taking place because King had not been involved or consulted. The injunction was denied. Later on, King was to have his own successes against Warren in court, but for the moment Warren felt he had scored a major victory. Just in case King felt that Warren owed him anything, and to rub in his triumph, Warren ordered yet another mountain-climbing, river-crossing Hummer, and sent it direct to King's office in Fort Lauderdale.

All battle-lines had been drawn: Brendan versus Riath, Warren versus King, Naseem versus Kelley.

# CHAPTER TWENTY-FOUR
## Sign on the Dotted Line

Two days before the fight, a document was delivered to Brendan in his room at the New York Palace hotel. Drawn up by a firm of London solicitors, it was a consultancy agreement between Naseem and himself which, he assumed, he was expected to sign.

As Brendan carefully read through the eleven pages, sixteen main clauses and many sub-clauses, and gradually worked out the import of the legal language, his feelings swung from anger to amusement. Anger because for Brendan the terms of the agreement amounted to servitude, and displayed contempt for his methods and beliefs. Amusement kicked in when Brendan realised the absurdity of the notion that anyone – be it Naseem or Riath, who had no doubt commissioned and dictated the terms of the agreement – could believe he would agree to its terms.

The agreement was to cover eight fights. The starting date had been left blank, but given the timing of the document's arrival in his room, Brendan figured that Riath hoped it would include the Kelley fight, and would therefore supersede the deal Brendan had struck with Naseem and his father. He knew Riath would have disliked that deal, partly because he had been excluded from the negotiation, and partly because Riath would have balked at paying Brendan 10 per cent of Naseem's purse.

Under the proposed eight-fight written agreement, Brendan would be responsible for Naseem's training, either at Brendan's gym or elsewhere, as directed. He would be required to give priority to Naseem over other boxers and obey Naseem's instructions. Brendan would not be allowed to speak to the press about Naseem without written permission and would be prevented from divulging any information not already publicly known. Brendan would ensure that his sons John and Dominic also signed secrecy agreements, and if they failed to adhere to them, would inform Naseem and help Naseem in any proceedings he might take against them. When the agreement terminated, Brendan would have to give up all documents, photographs and correspondence relating to Naseem, and would agree never to allow anyone to publish any photographs he had, including pictures of Naseem as a young boy. Brendan's payment would be £75,000 per fight.

On the afternoon of Friday 19 December, killing time in his room before setting off for Madison Square Garden, Brendan read through the document once more, shaking his head, but smiling. He was now beginning to find some satisfaction, even see some advantage in it. There it was in black and white, everything he had said about how he had been treated, how he was expected to kowtow, to obey orders like a servant. If people didn't believe him, he had the proof, provided by Riath himself.

Brendan put the document to one side, unsigned, and checked the contents of his brown bag. Adidas tracksuit and shoes, bandaging for Naseem's hands, white sticky tape, Vaseline, swabs, adrenalin in solution to apply to cuts, steel flat-iron to reduce swelling, scissors, white towel, and his small alarm clock. Brendan repacked the bag, put on his coat, and left the hotel at four o'clock. In his cap and coat, he walked to the arena, two blocks west, ten blocks south, along pavements crowded with office workers making their way home on a Friday evening. It was fight night and all thoughts of the agreement, of the betrayal he felt, had to be put aside. Whatever he thought of Riath, or of Naseem, he knew that if Naseem got licked, they were all licked – himself, Frank Warren, the gym, the system. For the moment, nothing mattered except Naseem winning.

# CHAPTER TWENTY-FIVE
## Let's Have a War

A few minutes after ten o'clock in the evening, New York time, on Friday 19 December 1997, Naseem stood at the top of the specially constructed illuminated ramp, the stairway from heaven that led to the ring erected in the very centre of the Madison Square Garden arena. He should have been on top of the world, the showman surveying his dominion, experiencing the exquisite thrill of achieving the summit. But Naseem was not himself.

At that moment, Kevin Kelley, in a frenzy, maddened by having to wait interminably for Naseem to arrive, paced the ring like a demented animal in a cage, jumping up on the ropes as if they were bars, and beckoning Naseem, his demon, to come and fight.

Frank Warren stood in the ring in a dinner suit, his neck prickly from the heat of the lights, fiddling with a wide, velvet bow-tie that was irritating his skin. He, too, stood at the symbolic height of his career, but he, too, was consumed by anxiety. Something had gone wrong with Naseem's entrance. Once Kelley had entered the ring conventionally, in a hooded dressing-gown, the lights had dimmed for the first sight of Naseem, high up at one end of the arena behind a screen, in silhouette. Warren had been looking forward to Naseem's entrance almost as much as to the fight itself. If such showbusiness flourishes caught on in American boxing as they had in Britain, widening the audience by enticing the hip, Warren would have made his mark and stolen a march on the other promoters, notably the self-proclaimed emperor of hype, Don King.

All heads turned to Naseem, all 12,000 of them, including celebrity guests such as Evander Holyfield, the world heavyweight champion, Pierce Brosnan, whose latest James Bond film had just opened in the city, and Donald Trump, New York's modern man of property.

Warren watched and smiled as Naseem performed a kind of octopus dance, all dangling and writhing limbs. Warren smiled and Naseem danced. But as Naseem kept dancing, and dancing, Warren's smile tightened. Naseem was supposed to burst through the screen. Why was he still dancing? What was going on up there? HBO and Sky timed their programmes to the second. The contracts contained every kind of penalty clause for non-appearance or late appearance. On and on Naseem went. But he was hardly dancing. He was going through the motions, as awkward as a vicar in a disco. Something was wrong with Naseem. Why didn't he come through the screen? And as Warren stood, impotent in the face of disaster, the thought crossed more than a few minds that perhaps Naseem was paralysed by fear. And when, finally, Naseem broke through the screen and stood to survey the Garden, he knew, Warren knew, everyone knew that the much-vaunted, spectacular, Princely entrance had been a flop.

Johnny Nelson stood at the bottom of the ramp, from where he and Clifton Mitchell and a few other minders were to escort Naseem to ringside. Nelson was worried, too. The most relaxed and reliable of camp-members, he had known Naseem almost from the moment the three Hamed brothers first walked into Brendan's gym. Nelson had a pretty good idea of what might have gone wrong with Naseem's entrance. He had been standing next to Naseem in the dressing room when the man from Madison Square Garden went through the routine – how long Naseem was to dance, when he was to break through the screen, when the smoke would start, how he was to go down the ramp – and Nelson could see that Naseem wasn't listening, he was going 'yeah, yeah', but he wasn't taking it in.

There hadn't been a rehearsal, as there always was in Britain, and because Naseem hadn't paid attention, a classic cock-up, born of miscommunication, ensued. Naseem waited for the signal from the man who was going to start the smoke, and the man waited for Naseem to come through the screen before starting the smoke.

But even before the endless dance, Nelson sensed something was amiss. In the dressing room Naseem had been subdued, and even before that, in the days leading to the fight, Nelson had noticed that rather than insisting on being the centre of attention, Naseem was quiet and withdrawn, wandering off on his own for hours.

Brendan, waiting by the ring, was concerned as well. Naseem's preparation had not been ideal. He had trained hard during the past week – too hard, showing off in the Blue Velvet, going ten, twelve rounds on the pads with John rather than tapering off his training. Yet even though Naseem had been within three pounds of the nine-stone featherweight limit ten days before the fight, he still had to lose some weight by shadow boxing in his hotel suite for ten rounds on the morning of the weigh-in, the very day before the fight. Then there had been a stupid problem with the gloves. That had shown how much Naseem was on edge.

The procedure for gloves in championship fights is tightly controlled. In New York, it is ultra tight. Stories about horseshoes and quick-drying cement may be apocryphal but tricks could be played. Panama Lewis, a well-known trainer, was imprisoned and banned from boxing for removing the padding from his fighter's gloves at Madison Square Garden in 1983.

As the champion's trainer, Brendan had first choice from three pairs of gloves approved by the New York State Athletic Commission. Brendan was happy with his choice. He was sure they would fit Naseem's hands well, that Naseem would be able to make a good fist. But when one of the commissioners brought the gloves Brendan had selected to Naseem's dressing room on the evening of the fight, Naseem decided he was not happy with them and that he wanted to change them, which was impossible and against the rules. What worried Brendan was not that Naseem didn't like the gloves, but that he was obviously unsettled.

Alma Ingle was in the sitting room in Newman Road. She had stayed up until three o'clock in the morning to watch the fight on Sky. She saw Naseem do his dance, and she saw that it went on and on until it petered out. When at last he broke through the screen, and she saw his face, she could tell that he was not right. She had known him since childhood and she could tell his moods, read his expressions. He looked lost, alone, and although, after everything that had happened, she could not be counted among his supporters or sympathisers, she felt sorry for him.

Naseem stood at the top of the ramp. The music was still blaring but it was drowned out by human chanting, rhythmic and insistent but difficult to interpret. Some shouted support, 'Naseem, Naseem', some shouted with venom, 'Kelley, Kelley', until Madison Square Garden was like the inside of a drum. The ring below awaited. Naseem was irritated. The entrance had gone wrong. The gloves were annoying. Struggling to make the weight had been annoying. The whole business with Brendan not talking to him, walking out and wanting more money, had been annoying. But most disconcerting of all must have been the news concerning the one person close to him who had not travelled to New York.

Down below, almost everyone in his world was present. Brendan and Frank Warren were in the ring. His brothers Riath, Nabeel and Ali were at the bottom of the ramp ready to escort him, along with Johnny Nelson and Clifton Mitchell; the rest of his family – his parents and four sisters and his brother Murad – were at ringside. So, too, was Ryan Rhodes, his best mate, who no longer had an unbeaten record. The only person missing was Naseem's girlfriend, Eleasha. And that was the secret. Naseem had told his family in New York but no one else knew, yet. Eleasha was pregnant.

Naseem skipped down the ramp as two funnels sprayed confetti into the air in imitation of a ticker-tape parade. That part of the entrance, at least, went smoothly. But when Naseem reached floor level and the embrace of his brothers, friends and minders, the crowd was loud and hostile, close enough to touch. As the party moved off, with Naseem in the centre of the swarm, Johnny Nelson and Clifton Mitchell looked back and saw two security men run and jump on a youth with a close-shaven head. They knocked the youth down and held him to the floor. His right arm was outstretched, pinned, and in his hand he held a gun. The gun was grabbed and the youth dragged away. Nelson looked forward towards Naseem. It was all right. He hadn't seen it.

When Naseem climbed up the steps leading to the ring and stood on the ring-apron outside the ropes, he found he had another problem.

The ropes were higher than any he had previously flipped over, and he wasn't sure he could make it. Here was a fine dilemma: if he tried the flip and failed, as had happened once before in public, he would look ridiculous; but if he ducked through the ropes, everyone would know he had chickened out. He had to do it. Naseem placed his gloved hands palm down on the top rope. He prepared for the effort, jumping up and down to get a spring from the canvas, and launched himself into the air, turning a full somersault and landing inside the ring. But he couldn't check his momentum, and although the ring was crowded with officials, he ran straight into Kevin Kelley.

In the last few suffocating seconds before the fight began, the time when taking a normal breath requires a conscious effort, Naseem and Kelley stood eyeball to eyeball as the ring announcer with the bouffant hair and prophetic delivery addressed the 'thousands in attendance and millions watching across the world', his speech accelerating as he introduced the champion 'from Sheffield, England, fighting out of the blue corner: weighing one hundred and twenty-six pounds, he has a record of twenty-eight wins, twenty-six coming by way of knockout, he is the undefeated WBO featherweight champion of the world, PRINCE NASEEEEEEEEM HAMED!'

Naseem cupped a boxing glove and spoke directly into Kelley's ear. 'You don't run.'

'I won't run.'

'We'll see who's got the best chin.'

'You're on.'

It was Naseem's second invitation for Kelley to stand and fight. At the weigh-in, the day before, he had said: 'Let's come out and we'll have a war in the first round.'

'You've got a deal,' Kelley had replied.

However public an event it may be, a fight between two men remains a private affair. Naseem and Kelley had agreed their own total-aggression pact. They had decided on a brawl, a trial by strength, rather than a boxing match. For Kelley, who had watched at ringside in England as Naseem demolished Tom Johnson and Jose Badillo, slugging it out was probably a good idea, his best chance to win.

For Naseem, such recklessness bordered on the suicidal. Brendan's advice, repeated and agreed by Naseem over several days, was that he must use the tactics that had served so well against Badillo – single shots, using the jab to break up the man before risking combinations. But Brendan's words were wasted. Naseem wasn't listening. He wasn't thinking about his fortune and prospects, or those of his family. He wasn't thinking about how far he had come and how much he had to lose. He was back in the playground and this was a tear-up.

It was madness, but then it was such madness that elevated Naseem from the ordinary and gave him the unpredictability that made him theatrically irresistible. And perhaps his reaction to all the faction-fighting and strife around him was to fight without care or caution, to escape.

At the first bell, clang, Naseem rushed out of his corner and swung a right hook, trying to knock off Kelley's head. Kelley had rushed forward too, and he had swung a right of his own. Both missed. But both were keeping to the bargain. Naseem took the southpaw stance and jabbed with his right hand, hard shots that were intended to hurt rather than find the range. Kelley, also southpaw, boxing in an intense, bobbing style with his hands held either side of his face, avoided them without trouble, and opened up himself with the right. Naseem, standing still in centre-ring, slipped Kelley's lead and gave an exaggerated shrug of his shoulders to emphasise his command. It was his last gesture of self-assurance, for the fighters and the crowd were soon consumed in the shocking, jolting violence of an earthquake. Single shots, Brendan had said. But when Naseem mounted his first really promising attack, forcing Kelley to cover up in a neutral corner, he could not resist opening up two-handed, blazing shots to head and body. Kelley seemed to bend and slump as if he had been hurt to the body, but he was the one with his wits about him. As Naseem emptied both guns like an over-excited gunslinger, Kelley took half a step forward, switched to the orthodox stance and threw one punch, a long right hand. Naseem was not merely blind to it, but unaware even of the possibility of its existence. When Daniel Alicea knocked him down in Newcastle, and Tom Johnson caught him in London, Naseem had seen the punches coming, and had managed to diminish their force and surprise by riding the impact. Kelley's punch, the worst he had ever received, arrived without warning. The lights were on, the lights were out, and Naseem was lifted and thrown backwards, dumped on his back, flattened. Naseem may have heard the count. He may have heard the uproar, the wild yelling of those who desired his comeuppance, the shock of the crowd, 12,000 shocks and one, but if his senses were jangled, his instincts were strong. Blood-drained and climbing through treacle, he rose to his feet, raised his gloves and went back to fighting.

'Don't go looking for him. Work off the jab,' said Brendan at the end of the first round, when Naseem sat on his stool in the corner. It wasn't easy for Brendan to know what to say. He needed five minutes to tell Naseem that he was circling the ring in the wrong direction, anticlockwise on to Kelley's left hand; that he was holding his hands down by his side and switching stance when he was in range, which was why Kelley was able to catch him almost at will; that he was using combinations instead of concentrating on the jab; that he was boxing like a novice.

Naseem had entered territory that was wholly unfamiliar. He was used to getting hit occasionally. Jose Badillo had caught him twice in seven rounds. Daniel Alicea had caught him three times and knocked him down; Tom Johnson had had his moments too. But Kelley was hitting him again and again, finding the target with almost every attack. Some credit had to go to Kelley. He was proving much faster than Naseem had imagined possible. (Indeed, when Naseem first saw a video of Kelley in action he dismissed him as 'slow'.) Kelley had done his homework so well that he was punching not to where Naseem's head was when the punch was thrown, but to where it was when the punch arrived.

It was not just that Naseem had never taken so many shots to the head. It was unheard of for any of Brendan's boxers, even those far inferior to Naseem, to take so many shots. That was why Brendan's boxers all retired with their faces and their minds intact. By choosing tactics that allowed Kelley to hit him so frequently, Naseem was inviting the most serious damage. Naseem took a left after a minute of the round, yet another punch to the head, and was thrown off balance, touching the canvas with his glove. Technically, it was a knockdown, and the referee should have given a mandatory count of eight. But before the referee could intervene, Naseem got to his feet, with his back to Kelley and his gloves dangling by his side, and turned into terrible trouble. His jaw was a defenceless, slow-moving target. Kelley swiped with his right hand, as easy as patting a child, and Naseem was knocked down for the second time.

When Naseem was upright again, it was clear that he was in dreadful danger. His legs, the mainspring of his power and movement, had become feeble and disconnected, strangers to his brain. He tried to step nicely, to look lively, but only made his condition more obvious, his legs so lax, his steps so drunken that the knowing ones at ringside murmured what is usually a knell: 'His legs have gone.'

Naseem's father, who had a seat a few rows back from the ring, stood up and shouted amid the mayhem. Riath was standing as well, apparently in shock. Frank Warren, sitting in the centre of the front row, shouted 'Keep them up!' Brendan, in the corner, prayed that Naseem's legs would begin to function before another punch knocked him out.

It might have been mad to begin with, but slugging it out had become Naseem's only course. With nothing but instinct to call upon, he attacked. He took yet another punch to the head, ignored it, and punched back, both hands, forcing Kelley to cover up in a neutral corner. It was a minor success, for it proved that whatever else had gone, Naseem's fighting spirit was intact, and it bought time for recovery.

The benefit soon came. In the moment of his greatest peril, Naseem found the most important single punch of his career. With a minute left of the second round, Kelley seemed to be drawing breath, waiting to assemble his next attack. Naseem had found steadiness and obedience in his legs. For the first time since the opening moments of the fight there was an interlude of scientific boxing, both men circling with care. Kelley stepped into range and pawed out a jab with his right hand. But Naseem's counter, a straight right hand through the centre of Kelley's defence, arrived first. It was the simplest punch but deadly, too fast for Kelley to react, too accurate for Kelley to absorb. It struck the point of Kelley's chin and sent him immediately to the canvas.

Kelley was not badly hurt. He lay on his back for a second, shaking his head and smiling, before smartly getting back to his feet. The punch's significance was not physical but symbolic. Hitherto, one man had been hitting, hurting, destroying the other; now they had both been down and they had each put the other down. And now the ring contained two desperate men, both dangerous, both fragile. Naseem, at last, was in the fight.

The third round was unique in containing no knockdowns. The fourth had three. Although Kelley continued to catch Naseem at long range, Naseem had imperceptibly and gradually become the predator. He had begun to concentrate, to look for the kill. His first chance came midway through the round. Naseem caught Kelley with a double left hook, the first striking the side of Kelley's face, and the follow-up so fast that Kelley was hit again as he fell. Kelley was up at the count of six, looking suddenly old but knowing that it was his turn to fight for survival. He had a brief, hollow success, when he launched a counter and Naseem gyrated out of the way and appeared to touch the canvas with his right glove. The referee gave a standing count as Naseem shook his head in protest. Knockdown or not, it made no difference. Naseem was in control. He had found his timing and he had a tired man in front of him. He let Kelley come to him, and allowed him to throw a left hook. Naseem watched it, and drew just slightly away before delivering the classic riposte, a chopping right hand, the delayed counter, the punch that has a terrible effect because its victim is moving on to it. Kelley fell and could not beat the count.

John Ingle, who had been in the corner with Brendan, was the first to reach, embrace and lift Naseem. Naseem's brothers and father, and Frank Warren, were not far behind. The fear of what might happen, of what was happening in front of them, of Naseem getting hurt and a fortune floating past beyond their grasp, had been replaced by a flood of emotion. The emotion was relief.

All around the arena, arguments had started. Scuffles broke out. For some, including the HBO executives and commentators, the fight had proved Naseem's heart and power. 'The kid's the real thing, he's pure theatre.' For others, little had been proved but the flaws in Naseem's boxing. 'How can a guy with no defence compare himself with Muhammad Ali?'

Brendan and Naseem knew the truth. It was Naseem's worst fight, his first acquaintance with the deep badness of boxing. Finding a way to the shore from such awful adversity had been his finest achievement, but he should never have been so close to drowning. Foolishness had brought peril; fighting instinct had saved him. Those elements would no doubt fight each other again and again, and one day the result might be different.

When Brendan made it through the crowd to the dressing room, Naseem and his brothers, with Johnny Nelson and the others, were already there. There were no pretences and no celebrations in that bare room. It was like a morgue. Brendan looked straight at Naseem. If he had needed to speak, he might have told Naseem that he had never boxed so badly, that he was an idiot, that he had been lucky to get away with it, that he had been an inch from destruction, that once again he hadn't listened. But Brendan only needed to shake his head and smile. Naseem gave a quiet laugh and for a second looked straight at Brendan. It was enough to show, Brendan was sure, that Naseem knew exactly what he was thinking, and that although he wouldn't say it, even if he was offered all the world, he knew Brendan was right.

# POSTSCRIPT

The end of the partnership between Brendan and Naseem came so quietly and with such anticlimax — all passion spent — that it was like burying a body that had long been dead.

A fortnight before Christmas 1998, at lunchtime on a Tuesday, Brendan was sitting in his front room in Newman Road with his wife, Alma, and two of his children, John and Tara. It had been five-and-a-half weeks since Naseem's thirty-first professional fight, against Wayne McCullough in Atlantic City, and Brendan had not been paid his trainer's fee. Alma had been chasing up the money, and had sent an invoice to Naseem's office, but had been fobbed off with excuses.

'I reckon they're not going to pay you,' she said.

'No, they've got to,' said Brendan. 'Come on, John, let's go up to Naz's place.'

When Brendan and John arrived at Naseem's house on the other side of Sheffield, Naseem was in the kitchen with his wife, Eleasha, and their baby son, Sami Naseem Salem Hamed. Naseem, who had been somewhat caught off guard, suggested they should talk at the office, Prince House, the impressive headquarters of Naseem Hamed Enterprises, just down the road.

An hour later, in the Prince House boardroom, with Brendan and John on one side, and Naseem, his father and his brother Nabeel on the other, discussion about Brendan's payment for the McCullough fight quite naturally evolved into negotiations for divorce. In fact, it was almost a race between Brendan and Naseem to utter the fateful words.

'Pay me what you owe me and then you go your way and I'll go mine,' said Brendan.

'We were going to say that,' said Naseem.

They were, too. Naseem produced an agreement for Brendan to sign. The burden of it was that in consideration of payment of £75,000 for Brendan's services as trainer for the McCullough fight, Brendan agreed not to divulge any confidential information about Naseem. Brendan signed it, a joint statement was agreed upon for the press, and Brendan left to go home with a cheque in his hand.

What had finally killed the partnership? Well, this book hadn't helped. It had been conceived as a neutral account and exploration of the relationship between Brendan and Naseem. But when it was published in Britain in September 1998, it had the effect of a hand grenade.

Naseem was furious with Brendan for 'betraying' him, for revealing intimacies that should have remained as confidential between boxer and trainer as between doctor and patient. Naseem said publicly that Brendan was 'totally and utterly money oriented, money motivated' and declared that Brendan had never trained him properly. He took to calling Brendan 'Judas'.

Naseem did not sack Brendan immediately. Instead, he tried to present himself as a new man who had grown through marriage and the birth of his son. Naseem wanted to prove himself more mature than Brendan, to 'forgive but not forget'. But when he fought McCullough, he seemed even more disturbed than he had been when he fought Kevin Kelley. He arrived in Atlantic City three days late, to the fury of HBO, and concluded a public workout by verbally attacking members of the media. The fight, according to one New Jersey radio show host, showed that Naseem was 'a total bum and proof that Brits can't box'. Naseem failed to knock out McCullough as promised and danced at range to a points victory. Between rounds, Naseem refused to listen to Brendan's advice in the corner and even pushed him away.

When they next met, five-and-a-half weeks later in Sheffield, they parted, and the immediate feeling was of relief, of freedom. Naseem would have to find another trainer and another gym. That wouldn't be difficult. But it wouldn't be the same. Brendan went home and wandered over to the gym, pushing open the heavy black door. It was as busy as ever.

# ACKNOWLEDGEMENTS

Although the foregoing is in no way 'authorised', I must chiefly thank Brendan Ingle and Naseem Hamed for their story, and their help and forbearance over many years.

I am also grateful to many others who were generous with their time and memory, among whom were Alma Ingle, John Ingle, Frank Warren, Nabeel Hamed, Riath Hamed, Johnny Nelson, Ryan Rhodes, Steve Bunce, Jon Thaxton, Paul Griffin and Daniel Teasdale.

I owe further debts (figuratively) to David Walsh and John Milne for planting the seed; Caroline Dawnay, my agent, for enthusiasm far beyond professional requirements; Rachel Cugnoni, of Yellow Jersey Press, for high-class editing and advice that brought substantial improvements; Beth Humphries for excellent copy-editing; Chris Smith for his wonderful pictures; and June Williamson for everything.